To: Sharon —
To God Be The
Glory!

D1491015

MY
JOHN
3:16

The Story of How My
17-Year-Old Son's Stroke
Changed Our Lives Forever

VICTORIA AND
JOHN MICHAEL NIGHT

Vickie:

This book is dedicated to my three amazing children.

Ryan, you are the best daughter and sister anyone could ask for. You are so strong and have such a big heart. I am in awe of you.

Ben, you have had to grow up way too quickly. You are an awesome brother and Ryan and John Michael are so lucky to have you. I am so proud of the young man you are becoming.

John Michael, you are our hero.

John Michael:

It's hard to dedicate this book to just one person (besides my mom) or a group of people, but I have to go with the Hannan family and Mercer men's lacrosse.

For all you have done and continue to do,
I cannot thank you enough.

No matter what, you always believe in
and are there for me.

Table of Contents

Introduction 1

Chapter 1: The Beginning of the End...................................5

Chapter 2: I Remember That Day 8

Chapter 3: Buzz Lightyear Becomes a Little Chief................9

Chapter 4: Living His Best Life 15

Chapter 5: If Each Day is a Gift, Can I Return This One?...17

Chapter 6: Yes, I Still Make My Kids Breakfast...................19

Chapter 7: And Then the Bell Rang 20

Chapter 8: Starting the Day Off Right 22

Chapter 9: Waiting for the Text..23

Chapter 10: Helpless...25

Chapter 11: Sober Drunk..26

Chapter 12: The Nightmare Begins 27

Chapter 13: The ER...34

Chapter 14: Lifeless..36

Chapter 15: Tests... and More Tests 38

Chapter 16: Locked-In – Trapped in His Body..................42

Chapter 17: We Need a Miracle 47

Chapter 18: I Can't Be That Mom...........................57

Chapter 19: Waking Up to Reality 61

Chapter 20: A Pile of Brokenness 65

Chapter 21: The Squad 71

Chapter 22: Time to Get to Work...........................75

Chapter 23: Learning to Communicate.......................81

Chapter 24: Christmas Celebration 84

Chapter 25: Believe 88

Chapter 26: The Good Shepherd.............................90

Chapter 27: Where is God? 92

Chapter 28: And So It Began 98

Chapter 29: The First Outing.............................107

Chapter 30: The Look of a Warrior 110

Chapter 31: Healing and Miracles........................113

Chapter 32: Waiting, Waiting, Waiting 115

Chapter 33: Building a New Community 119

Chapter 34: Friends......................................123

Chapter 35: The Story of '24' 128

Chapter 36: Brad Pitt and Jesus 131

Chapter 37: Good and Evil 133

Chapter 38: With a Little Help from Our Friends.............135

Chapter 39: JMStrong24...139

Chapter 40: The Many Blessings of Our Community 142

Chapter 41: Progress 144

Chapter 42: Attitude is Everything..................................148

Chapter 43: Rising Up 152

Chapter 44: Coming of Age 154

Chapter 45: The Prom..156

Chapter 46: Some Things are Just Not Fair 159

Chapter 47: Places to Go..161

Chapter 48: Going Home 166

Chapter 49: The Parade..170

Chapter 50: Not a Second Wasted....................................176

Chapter 51: Graduation 182

Chapter 52: Are You Listening, God? 186

Chapter 53: The Beach...192

Chapter 54: Our New Normal 195

Chapter 55: Our First Thanksgiving.................................204

Chapter 56: The Test..207

Chapter 57: Running 209

Chapter 58: A Downward Spiral 212

Chapter 59: Moses and Joshua 216

Chapter 60: Seashells...220

Chapter 61: Precious Children 224

Chapter 62: Determination...226

Chapter 63: A Day in My Life...229

Chapter 64: Communicating 235

Chapter 65: I Will Walk Again.......................................238

Thoughts from our good friend, Scott Levitt................. 243

Thoughts from John Michael's Dad, Mick..................... 246

Chapter 66: Tattoo...249

Chapter 67: God is Good..251

Acknowledgements 253

Notes from John Michael's Therapists 257

Stroke Resources..267

Follow the Miracle...270

Introduction

I am by no means a writer. Let's just say that in school, writing was not my best subject. The idea for a book began when I started writing the updates for my son, John Michael, about six weeks after his stroke. Many have encouraged me to write a book, so here I am writing. Most days I am not even sure what I am writing about. I sometimes feel like Esther from the Bible when Mordecai said to her, "And who knows but that you have come to your royal position for such a time as this." Now don't get me wrong – by no means do I think there is anything remotely royal about the position I was forced into, but I truly believe John Michael's story needs to be told, if for no other reason than to give hope to those who can't seem to find any.

If I've heard it once, I've heard it a thousand times – kids don't stroke. Well, I am here to tell you they do. Unfortunately, my son is not the only one. I have met, spoken with, or read many stories of kids who have suffered massive strokes. It isn't common, but it does happen. It needs to be on "the list" of things to check for instead of defaulting to just the symptoms. Our hope and prayer is to raise awareness and hopefully spare another child and family from this horrible outcome.

There are many stories woven within this one larger story. I wrestle with so many questions. Should I touch on all of them? Do I focus on one? Will anyone ever read this? Do I pour out my heart at the risk of offending or hurting someone's feelings? Where do I even start? If you Google "how to write a book," some recommend starting at the end. Well, I am happy to say that as of this moment in time, our end has not yet arrived.

So I thought it only made sense to start at the beginning, but I quickly realized that the beginning is actually an end – an end to a life we once knew and loved, an end to dreams and goals fulfilled, an end to a part of myself. I realized I had to own my story in order to truly heal. My hope and prayer is that since you picked up this book, you will find within these pages faith and love and hope. I hope you will see His handprints throughout this tragedy, and I pray you see that no matter how bad your situation may be, someone always has it worse.

Reading through the text messages I sent during those few days still makes me cry. The fear, the worry, the panic, the distress, and magnitude of it all was evident in each text. Within every text were the words, "I am freaking out!" I am so grateful that I have these texts. It helps fill in the gaps when I can't remember, which is really a double-edged sword. I want to know and remember, but reliving it is excruciating. From these messages, I remember how scared and upset I was, and John Michael as well. We tried to keep it honest and real, and as positive as we could, and we didn't sugar coat anything for him. One doctor would always tell him, "I'm not going to blow smoke up your ass."

The hardest part was not having any answers, like when he asked, "How long will I be like this?" No one, then or now, can answer that question. We quickly learned that every stroke is different, every locked-in case is different, and every brain heals differently. This was John Michael's stroke, his healing, his race. There is no blueprint or prescription for recovery. We just hang on to the fact that if you don't use it, you lose it. This is why, to this day, he has therapy five days a week.

My faith has always been important to me and has seen me through some pretty tough times, but I can honestly say it has been my rock, my anchor, my only hope when all the odds have been against John Michael. I hope that in this story you will find a way to love the cross you bear. Although there are many times you do not like it and feel as if you can't carry it a step further, it is your cross. It was meant for you, and God will provide you with the strength you need to keep going.

3

I would not trade my life for anyone else's, because while my cross may be unbearably heavy at times, it is beautifully made by the Creator – just for me.

CHAPTER 1

The Beginning of the End

(Vickie)

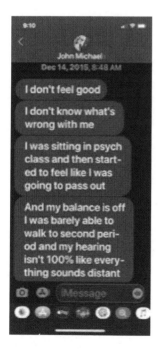

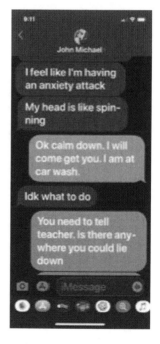

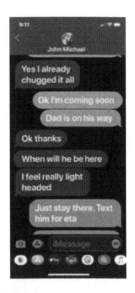

That is how it all began.

I received a text from my son at 8:48 a.m. on that fateful Monday morning. It would be his last text to me for over a year.

It started out as a typical morning. I awoke at 5:45 a.m., made my coffee, and headed out back for my quiet time with God. I remember thanking Him for a great time with my sisters and mother as we had celebrated her 80th birthday in Savannah over the past weekend. While I was out of town, John Michael played in what would be his very last lacrosse tournament with a team he played for in the off season, Ponte Vedra. He played well on Saturday, but Sunday he said he was too tired to play and needed to study for exams the following week. In hindsight, that decision might have saved his life.

CHAPTER 2

I Remember That Day

(John Michael)

I remember everything about that day. I'm going to tell you all of it, down to the yellow-collared shirt I was wearing, not because I want to, but because I am called to. It's time that my story, the whole story, is shared. For the longest time, people were amazed that my memory was not affected by the stroke. I'll be the first to admit the beginning was hazy and the journey has been incredibly long and difficult up to this point, but I will never forget when I walked in and out of school for the last time.

CHAPTER 3

Buzz Lightyear Becomes a Little Chief

(Vickie)

Technically, he is my John 3/16, but over the last few years, John Michael has shown me the true meaning of John 3:16. John Michael Night was born on March 16, 1998. I have always joked that he came out of the womb smiling and hasn't stopped since. He stole my heart the minute he was born. Growing up with three sisters and already the mother of a daughter, I was so excited to have a boy. He had such a gentle demeanor. The first time I held him I was immediately drawn to his sweet eyes. They just drew me in. They radiated such peace and happiness. His eyes were blue for the first four years, but then turned more green than blue. Even after having three kids, I am still amazed that you can look at someone and hold them for the first time and just immediately love them so much.

John Michael rarely cried as a baby. He slept through the night at eight weeks. He was the perfect infant. I could take him anywhere; he would just sit there so content. He was, and still is, my easygoing, don't-take-life-so-seriously child. We had an immediate bond and he had me wrapped around every little finger. His blonde hair, his chubby little legs, and his infectious smile made everyone who met him love him. His big sister loved him so much she would squeeze him until he was red in the face. He was her little "baby doll." She was the proud big sister and took great care of him. To this day, she still does. He will always be her little Jon Jon. When John Michael learned to speak, saying John Michael was quite a mouthful, so he would call himself Jon Jon. That name lasted through middle school when he finally outgrew it.

John Michael was full of life. He started to walk at 10 months — actually, he ran more than walked. When he found an interest in something, it became a passion. When John Michael was three, he loved Buzz Lightyear. Almost daily he would dress up in his costume and make everyone call him Buzz. He had every Buzz Lightyear toy they made. My dear friend Lorrie even brought a life-size Buzz Lightyear balloon to his PICU room.

He also never went anywhere as a toddler without a handful of Thomas the Tank Engine trains. He spent hours playing at his train table. One Easter he actually came downstairs dressed as Harry Potter for our Easter egg hunt. He had such a great imagination and would easily entertain himself for hours with his imaginative play and fascination with these characters.

And so it became with lacrosse. John Michael picked up his first lacrosse stick when he was nine years old and immediately fell in love with the sport. From that moment on, he did anything and everything to improve his game. During those first few years playing lacrosse, he was never one of the best or the star of the team. He was a solid player who played hard and fought for play time. It wasn't until eighth grade that his game took a turn, and he became one of the best at his position. John Michael was a face-off specialist, and he was self-taught. He participated in many clinics and worked out with other face-off guys over the years, but it was the countless hours he spent in our yard working to perfect his game that took him to the next level. When his sister came home from college she would ask, "Why is he always outside practicing lacrosse?" The answer was simple: he had goals and dreams that he wanted badly and was working toward.

We never pushed John Michael; we didn't have to. He was self-motivated and committed to whatever he set his mind to accomplish. He was always a team player, competitive mostly with himself. When he would face-off against someone, he would figure out what the other guy was doing, then find a way to beat him. Lacrosse became his life. It became part of his identity. He was a "lax bro."

It was in ninth grade that he started talking about his goal of playing at the collegiate level. In the beginning of that year, he went on his class trip to the mountains of North Carolina. He was no stranger to those mountains. He had been going to summer camp in those mountains since first grade. That is where he first encountered Jesus – at the top of the mountains.

Camp Ridgecrest was a special place for John Michael. It was a faith-based camp and so much more. It was a place where boys could be boys. They played outside all day and got dirty. They learned what it means to be a gentleman and how to love and serve God. Most of his summers, once he reached middle school, were filled with lacrosse tournaments, but he always made time for camp. Every summer when we would get there to drop him off, he would say, "I'm home." He developed many lifelong friendships in that camp and learned what it meant to live out his faith.

While at camp, the boys had an opportunity to get promoted in rank. You earned a promotion with good behavior, being helpful, being a leader, good attitude, and so on. The highest ranking at camp was that of Little Chief. It was no easy feat to become a Little Chief. You first had to get "tapped out," which meant you were chosen to complete the Little Chief test. The test began at 11:15 p.m. The candidates were brought down and read the Little Chief Charge. They were then led in prayer and walked to the trail where they were given an hour to collect wood. At the end of the hour, they struck their first of two matches. If their first match did not light, they were given an additional half-hour to collect more wood and restructure their fire. They then had to light their second match. If their second match did not light, they failed the Little Chief Test. They could not use paper, straw, leaves, or any other kindling to start their fire. If they were successful in building the fire, they continued to feed the flame and keep the fire burning until 6:00 a.m., at which point they extinguished their fires. Then they were driven to the base of the mountain which they ran up at a pace determined by the Little Chiefs. There was a person in the front who they could not pass and a person in the back who they could not be passed by. They could not take any shortcuts, walk around corners, or break the pace of the run. If they fell, they had to get up again immediately and continue.

Upon reaching the top of the mountain, they were led in a devotion and given an opportunity to focus on the One who would continue to be with them throughout the day. They were driven back to camp and allowed to shower and eat breakfast before writing an essay entitled, "What Camp Ridgecrest Means to Me." The essay had to be coherent, relevant to the subject, and 1,500 words in length. After lunch, the candidates performed hard labor such as moving logs, making torches, and drying sawdust. The hard labor continued until 6:00 p.m.

One of the hardest parts of the test was the silence ban. From the moment the candidates stepped off the porch until the moment the test was over (approximately 18 hours), they could not make any audible noise. They could not speak or even grunt. Notes of communication were allowed only to members of the Central Staff and to Little Chiefs. The Silence Ban was a very important part of the Little Chief test because it tested the candidates' own self-control. If a candidate failed any portion of the test at any time, he was honor bound to turn himself in. I explain this in detail because many may get tapped out, but few actually passed the test.

John Michael failed his first time. He turned himself in for making a noise. But the next year, he passed. When he was writing college essays, this is what he wrote about. It's not only an honor in his mind, but it showed his strength, character, and determination to us very early on.

CHAPTER 4

Living His Best Life

(Vickie)

In November 2015, John Michael signed his National Letter of Intent to play D1 Lacrosse at Mercer University. Four years prior, in a letter that he wrote as a class project, he had set out some goals for his life. Receiving a D1 scholarship was one of his predictions, further proving that he could accomplish anything he set his mind to.

Signing day was easily one of the best days of his life, and I was so proud of him. We were all excited. His sister came home to surprise him, and we took his brother, Ben, out of school early so we all could be there. His grandparents came into town as well. We arrived a few minutes before the ceremony. The upper school had an assembly and brought the athletes who would be signing letters onto the stage. After the assembly, they sat at a table in the front where everyone could see. John Michael sat next to one of his best friends, Jared, who was signing to play baseball at Florida State University. It was an extra special day watching him sit there in his orange Mercer shirt next to Jared wearing his garnet and gold.

After the ceremony, we had a celebratory lunch with the family. That night, we had our own signing party with his friends, coaches, and all of our family friends who had watched him grow up. There was such peace in my heart. I felt so proud that everything he had worked so hard for was coming to fruition. Every parent can say that to see your child pour their blood, sweat, and tears into achieving a goal and then accomplish it is easily one of the greatest joys of parenting.

Of course, Christmas was just around the corner. I was headed to Savannah on December 11th and knew I needed to be very organized for the holiday that year. I did not want to come home and have only a little over a week to get everything ready. Before I left, I had the tree up, my house all decorated, and some of the shopping finished. I just needed to buy a few more gifts, and I'd be all ready to relax and enjoy the holiday. I guess God had me prepared, because there would be no time for Christmas this year – certainly not the way I expected it.

Chapter 5

If Each Day is a Gift, Can I Return This One?

(John Michael)

Monday, December 14, 2015:

It was as normal a morning as I could ask for. I woke up feeling completely fine. No signs of anything. I had actually just played that weekend for Ponte Vedra High School, which would often pick me up for off-season tournaments since Trinity never had a solid club team. Anyway, I decided not to play on Sunday in preparation for midterms that week.

It was a Monday. It was the last regular school day before exams the next three days, arguably just a pointless review day. I knew a fair number of people who weren't even going to school that day, probably in anticipation of winter break, for the most part. I decided to attend anyway. I was up around 6:45 a.m., and I came downstairs to a wonderful omelet and toast made by my loving mother. People always criticized her and questioned why she still made us breakfast. "They're perfectly capable," people would say, to which she would reply, "Yes, but someday I won't get to, so I want to while I still can." Her God-like selflessness never ceases to amaze me.

I grabbed a bottle of water and was out the door around 7:20 a.m. I got to school around 7:40 a.m. I parked next to (and walked in with) my close friend Rowly Evans. Rowly was born the day after me, March 17, and our dads, who both went to high school in Winter Park, reconnected when they were looking at babies through the window at the hospital! Despite growing up near each other, Rowly and I actually met in North Carolina during our first year at Camp Ridgecrest. There we were in the same cabin with another life-long friend, Connor Corbett, who was from Myrtle Beach. If that's not divine intervention, I don't know what is.

So I made my way to advisory at 7:45 a.m. My advisor was Dennis Herron, the school principal, and more importantly, the father of my best friend, Jared Herron. Jared and I didn't grow close until high school, but once we did, we had a tight bond. We both shared a strong drive to succeed in our respective sports. Only a short month ago, we sat next to each other signing our National Letters of Intent.

8:00 a.m., first period: how was I supposed to know that in 45 minutes my life was going to change forever?

CHAPTER 6

Yes, I Still Make
My Kids Breakfast

(Vickie)

It was Monday, December 14th. I finished my quiet time, and at 6:45, woke up John Michael and his brother Ben for school while my husband, Mick, headed to the gym. It was the last week before Christmas break. My daughter Ryan was home from FSU and was happy to be able to sleep in. I made the boys omelets with bacon and toast for breakfast. At around 7:20 a.m., I said goodbye to John Michael, told him to drive safely, have a great day, and that I loved him, as I did every day. Little did I know it would be the last time he would walk out that door.

CHAPTER 7

And Then the Bell Rang

(John Michael)

My first period class was psychology. It's ironic that one of the topics we covered was neuroplasticity. I never could quite grasp the concept at the time, but now it's all I know. On that day, we were taking a test. The whole morning, I felt fine... until the bell rang.

I don't think anyone knows this story, not even my mom until she reads this. That day, in the moment, it didn't seem important. Then for a while, I wasn't able to communicate it, and once I could, it went back to being unimportant because I had bigger problems.

The exact moment the bell rang for the first period to be over, I felt it. It was 8:45 a.m. on the dot, and there was a sort of crick in the back of my neck. I know this may not have been what happened anatomically, but I remember the exact feeling. It felt as if something had burst and leaked at the base of my skull. I had just finished the test, and I needed to set my paper on the desk in the front of the room. When I stood up, I was immediately off balance. I also felt like I might pass out and everything sounded muffled and far away. Everyone was either turning in their papers or getting up to leave, so no one noticed that I stumbled my way up to the front desk with the help of a few chairs. I had no contact with the teacher. I just turned in my test and left with what I played off as a bad headache.

On my way to second period, I ran into my close friend Adam Hale. Adam and I were best described as the one-two punch of Trinity Prep lacrosse. If we weren't assisting each other on goals, he was my wingman on face-offs, picking up every ground ball I popped out to him. In the hall, we struck up a conversation. After a little bit, I brought up some of the symptoms I was feeling. I normally wouldn't share something like that, but it was really bothering me. His mother was a nurse, and he thought maybe it was blood sugar related. I told him I didn't think that was it because of the big breakfast I had eaten that morning. He wished me well, and we parted ways so we wouldn't be late for our next class. That is when I start texting my mom.

CHAPTER 8

Starting the Day Off Right
(Vickie)

I took Ben to school and drove into the chapel for morning Mass. Going to morning Mass was something I tried to make a part of my daily routine after dropping him off. I almost skipped it that morning. I had so much to do that day and really wanted to get in a good workout, but something was telling me I needed to go, so I went.

After Mass, I headed to the car wash with the goal of hitting the gym afterwards. I was walking inside to pay when I received John Michael's first text. My car had just entered the car wash. I was trapped.

CHAPTER 9

Waiting for the Text

(John Michael)

My second period class was photography. There were two rooms, and my teacher was in the other one because a lot of this class was freelance. So I had no contact with him for the five to 10 minutes I was in the room. By no means am I saying that either of these teachers should have approached me and asked what was wrong. They had no way of knowing what was going on, and given the circumstances, I was purposefully being kind of elusive. The pain had gotten bad enough to the point where I asked my mom to come get me.

She told me to drink some water, put my head down, and wait. Thank God both my parents were nearby. My dad was working and my mom was at the car wash, so she told him to come because he would get there first. My seat was close to the door in this class, too. I sat next to my buddy, Ryan Schaeffer, who would be the last person I talked to at Trinity. He also suggested that I drink water, and I showed him the empty bottle that I had downed once I started not feeling right.

By this point I texted my girlfriend at the time, Julia Smith, who went to New Smyrna High School. I assured her that I was going to be okay. I remember having my head down just waiting and praying for that text that my dad was close. As soon as it came, I was out the door without a word to anyone.

CHAPTER 10

Helpless

(Vickie)

I immediately called Mick, and he headed to school to pick John Michael up. Fortunately, we live in a small town, and the school is, at most, 15 minutes from his office. I sat there frantically texting John Michael and talking to Mick as he drove. I felt so helpless. Why was it taking so long? Looking back, I'm not sure why I did not call the school and have them check on him. I just knew in my heart that we had to get to him as soon as possible. As soon as my car was out, I headed to the school as well. When I arrived, John Michael was getting into Mick's car. He was visibly upset. We went to the closest ER, and that's when the nightmare began.

CHAPTER 11

Sober Drunk

(John Michael)

I have to make light of the situation and tell you, quite honestly, that I looked and felt drunk walking out of school (not that I would know what that's like or anything because underage high school seniors never drink – LOL).

Everything was slightly spinning, or at least I couldn't keep focus on one object, and I couldn't walk straight. I saw a faculty member I didn't recognize and tried to act as normal (or "sober") as possible. I casually nodded and hurried past, but I can only imagine what she was thinking.

My dad pulled up to the front of the school. I opened the car door and got in. As I sat down, I started getting upset. I didn't like how I was feeling or the fact that I wasn't fully in control of my body. Once my mom showed up and I started to calm down a little, we headed for the ER. This is where things get a little hazy and I start to lose track of time.

Chapter 12

The Nightmare Begins
(Vickie)

John Michael was able to walk into the ER. Although he was leaning a bit, he was still able to communicate fully. As we waited to go in the back, we talked about his weekend, if he had done anything, or if anything out of the ordinary had happened. He couldn't think of anything.

We were taken back in a room and the ER doctor came in to examine him. She diagnosed him with vertigo. After a few minutes, John Michael became nauseated and sick. They gave him medication for the vertigo. Up until that point, I was sitting there thinking, "Ok, we should be out of here in 30 minutes, and I can get to the gym and start my day."

But then something started to not feel right. I could see it in his eyes. My maternal instinct kept telling me something was so wrong. Nothing against dads, but moms sometimes just know things about their children that no one else could ever understand. I was not satisfied with the diagnosis, so I asked if they could at least do a CT scan. Mick and I went back with him to where they do the scans. It was so cold, and when we returned to his ER room, he immediately started shaking uncontrollably. We thought he was just cold. We covered him with warm blankets, but nothing helped.

Suddenly, he was unable to form words, and the shaking worsened. The nurse came in for us to sign discharge papers and, after looking at his condition and asking John Michael to sign (which, by the way, he couldn't do because he was only 17), she realized that something more was going on and called for the doctor. The ER doctor came back in. She felt this was an allergic reaction to the vertigo medication and said they would have to transfer him to the main hospital because they did not have a pediatric unit here. As we waited to be transferred, his condition began to deteriorate. I texted my sisters and my friends in my Bible study asking for prayer.

Memories from Vickie's sister, Big Maria

We had just returned from our mom's 80th birthday party in Savannah, Georgia. It was a Monday morning, and I was going about business as usual. I don't remember the exact time I got the call about JM, but it was in the morning. My sister, Little Maria, called to say JM was at the hospital with vertigo symptoms. Vickie had some texts from him saying he was dizzy, had a headache, and it felt like people were far away when speaking to him. She had been at the car wash and both she and Mick had gone to the school and taken him to the emergency room.

Memories from Vickie's sister, Mercedes

I was at work the morning that Vickie first texted and told us she had taken John Michael to the hospital. She said that he was given medicine for vertigo, and they had to transport him to the main hospital because he was 17.

Then I received a text from my sister, Little Maria (LM), that we should plan on going to Winter Park, but I held off, waiting to hear back from Vickie. Things seemed okay at this point. When I walked in the door from work, I received a frantic call from LM that I had to go now.

Memories from Vickie's sister, Little Maria

I will never forget that morning of December 14, 2015. I had woken up early as I was still jetlagged. I was thinking of all I had to do to get ready for Christmas before the rest of my family arrived from London and different parts of the U.S. I was living in London at the time with my husband and youngest daughter. We were planning to spend the holidays at our home in North Carolina with our three older daughters who were now living back in the U.S.

Vickie called and seemed very concerned as she was on her way to meet JM and Mick at school to take JM to the ER. She told me JM's symptoms and that she wasn't sure what was wrong with him. I told her to keep me posted. I tried to keep myself busy and not worry.

She kept calling me that day updating me. There was so much confusion as no one knew what was going on. In turn, I kept calling my other sisters and friends, anyone I could think of to ask what they thought could be wrong with JM. Nothing was adding up.

Memories from John Michael's sister, Ryan

December 14, 2015 – a day I will forever remember.

I had returned home for Christmas Break, all as normal, plans for regular traditions, my favorite time of the year! John Michael received his acceptance letter to FSU (although already committed to play lacrosse at Mercer, but still an accomplishment for our Nole-loving family). Ben had his annual Advent concert at SMM, Dad took us kids to a Magic game, all of us decorated the Christmas tree – Mom had all the decorations up as she always did. Just waiting for JM to finish his midterm exams so we could enjoy the holiday together!

The night before John Michael's life changed forever, I sat on his bedside as he was FaceTiming his girlfriend Julia and asked him if he was ready for his exams (of course, he mentioned he'd just started studying!). We caught up for a bit and then I let him prepare for his tests and get a good night's sleep.

The morning of December 14th, I slept in and woke up to find no one at home. I knew JM and Ben were at school. My dad was working and figured my mom was on a run. I had plans to meet several friends from home for brunch at The Broken Egg in the Winter Park Village, so I continued to go meet them. Once we wrapped up eating, we decided to walk around the shops, and it was then that I got the call from my dad.

"Hey Ry, I just wanted to let you know that Mom and I had to pick up JM from school, he is not feeling well – dizzy, nauseous, and off balance. Mom is with him at the Winter Park Hospital I am going to Walgreens to grab a few things; we are waiting to hear the results from a couple tests – they think it may be vertigo. I will keep you posted; try to stay calm, and if you could please pick up Ben from school, that would be a huge help. I'll call you as soon as we know more."

In that moment I could hear in my dad's voice the panic and worry. I knew he was staying strong for me, and all I could do was pray and lean on my friends. I too had to be strong for my younger brother Ben.

For the next couple hours I paced around my house and my friend Kelsey tried to keep me distracted. We talked in my backyard, went to the grocery store, and she even came with me to pick up Ben from school. I told Ben exactly what my dad had shared with me, because that's all I knew at that point. Ben, of course, was worried and asked when everyone would be coming home. I didn't know how to answer that.

I kept a brave face for Ben, for I had no idea what the next three days had in store for our family. Kelsey helped distract Ben while I checked in with my dad. That evening, I received an update about JM. Since he was 17 years old, they could not properly treat him at the WP Hospital; he was technically a pediatric patient, so they sent him in an ambulance to the Florida Hospital pediatric ICU. My dad mentioned JM was uncontrollably shaking and not fully conscious. The WP hospital had given him medicine for the vertigo and believed this was a bad reaction, so they immediately tried to flush out the medicine; this was not helping, according to my dad. They waited at Florida Hospital for several hours just wondering what is wrong while my brother continues to shake, and little did we know at the time, stroke.

Dad told me they were running tests and he would continue to update me, but they didn't want me to come yet – they didn't want me to see my brother like that because they knew I would fall apart.

Ultimately, my mom and JM had to stay the night in the PICU. With almost no answers, I took Ben to dinner, got him *ready for bed and school the next day, and tried to act as normal as possible. We saw my dad briefly that night so he could pick up clothes for my Mom, JM, and himself. I couldn't read him; we still had no clue what had happened or what was happening to JM.*

CHAPTER 13

The ER

(John Michael)

I started feeling a little better in the car because I walked into the ER (leaning a bit), sat down and waited to be admitted. The first nurse I saw did all the usual stuff. She took my vitals (which were normal) and asked me questions. When we were taken back to a room, the doctor came in and diagnosed me with vertigo. I had never even heard of that but shortly after, I started getting sick. They waited until my stomach calmed down to give me the medicine for vertigo, Meclizine. Not satisfied with what was happening, my mom asked them to do a CT scan. They took us back to do the test, and the room was absolutely freezing.

When we got back to the ER room, I started shaking uncontrollably. They covered me with blankets, but nothing was working. The nurses assumed it was a bad reaction to the medication and kept trying to get us to sign discharge papers.

One of them asked me to sign, and my mom said. "Oh no, he can't. He's only 17."

"I just want to see if he can," the nurse replied. I couldn't.

They decided that they would need to transfer me to the larger hospital which had a pediatric ICU. Meanwhile I could no longer form any words. I laid there, looking at my parents. The looks on their faces told me that they felt as helpless as I did.

At some point, the EMTs arrived and loaded me into the ambulance. By now, I couldn't speak at all, and it was incredibly hard to breathe. I'm pretty sure I had some type of oxygen mask on during the ride, but I motioned that I needed more as soon as we got there. The last thing I remember is the doors of the ambulance opening and being wheeled out on my stretcher.

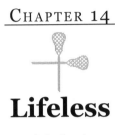

CHAPTER 14

Lifeless

(Vickie)

When the EMTs arrived at the ER to transport John Michael to the main hospital, it was evident that they also felt this was not a reaction to the vertigo medication. I overheard them speaking with the staff of the Pediatric ICU, explaining that they were bringing him straight in to examine him.

As soon as we arrived at the main hospital, John Michael signaled that he was having trouble breathing. They immediately took us to the PICU where they gave him some oxygen. At this point, he could no longer speak, and the shaking had worsened. He was sweating profusely, so much so that they had trouble keeping an IV in his arm. They were trying to get him stable to be able to start running tests. Nothing was helping. It felt like everyone was just standing around staring at him not knowing what to do.

I think this is when the shock began to set in. It was about 11:30 in the morning. For the next few hours, John Michael remained unconscious, for the most part, but he was still able to squeeze my hand. Throughout the night, he would have periods of rest followed by moments of shaking.

Mick and I stayed with him that night. He was hooked up to four IVs and several machines. We took turns sitting in the chair by him or resting on the couch in his room. I remember praying a verse that my friend had sent me, over and over. It was Psalm 57:1, "Be merciful, oh God, to John Michael. Be merciful to him, for You are his refuge. Hide him in the shadow of your wings until the path of destruction passes by." I longed to lay by him and make it all better. As he laid there, all I could see was his sweet little boy face – my little Jon Jon. Little did I know that would be the first of many nights sleeping in a chair watching and praying over him.

The following morning his body was lifeless.

CHAPTER 15

Tests... and More Tests
(Vickie)

The next day, they began running every test you could think of from an EKG to a spinal tap to an EEG to blood work for rare diseases. Every test came back normal. We couldn't understand how they had nothing. They were at a loss. At one point, they wanted me to believe my son had been doing synthetic drugs. Seriously, a straight-A D1-committed athlete would be doing drugs the week of midterm exams? They were grasping at straws because they could not figure out what was wrong. I always said that I did not want to be that naive parent who believes that their child "would never." So Mick and I started calling his friends. Every last one confirmed what we knew – John Michael would never do drugs. I was so angry that I even asked, but I knew it was better to be safe than sorry.

That night, the PICU doctor came in to examine him and said he felt locked-in. They would need to do a spinal MRI. I had no idea what that even meant.

One thing I loved about the hospital was that before they ran any test or procedures, someone always asked if they could pray over John Michael. This gave me such comfort. So at around 1:30 in the afternoon, when they wheeled him away for that four-hour spinal MRI, the prayers offered up for him comforted me.

Mick and I waited for John Michael to return to his room. It was the longest four hours of my life. We left for a bit to go across the street to Panera Bread. Walking outside to take a call from my sister, it was hard to talk between the sobs. Why couldn't they figure out what was wrong? Why isn't someone doing something? With all the advances in medicine, how in the world did they not have a clue? The answers to these questions were about to be revealed, but I wasn't remotely ready for them.

Memories from Vickie's sister, Big Maria

We continued to get updates for the next two days. Since JM was an athlete, young and strong, we felt like it would be okay. The doctors would figure this out, and he would be going home soon. The updates were confusing. Sometimes they sounded promising and other times more serious as his condition was not improving.

It went from vertigo to the meds they had given him, to "we have no idea!"

My sister LM and I had packed a bag on Monday so we would be ready to go down to Orlando on a moment's notice. We continued to get calls from Vickie about JM's status on Monday and Tuesday. By Wednesday we were feeling like maybe he had stabilized and was turning a corner, so we went shopping and out to lunch. It was close to Christmas and LM was getting her house ready for the holidays. We had just returned to her house and sat down for dinner when Vickie called with really bad news.

Memories from Vickie's sister, Little Maria

As the hours and then days went by, the panic and anxiety got stronger. JM's condition was deteriorating. I got friends of friends to call doctors they knew, trying anything and everything desperately trying to help my sister and nephew figure out what possibly could be happening.

The days were agonizing, each call from her more desperate, each call bringing more and more uncertainty. I wanted to do something but didn't know how to help. I made contingency plans to have my family meet me in Florida instead of spending Christmas in our home in North Carolina just in case we had to go down last minute to be with them.

Memories from John Michael's sister, Ryan

I barely slept that night. I woke up thinking it was all a dream. I'm pretty sure I called my dad 10 times throughout the night. I took Ben to school the next day and surrounded myself with close friends to keep distracted. I still didn't know much, I was praying they knew the answer about what had happened, that JM would be okay and that they'd be coming home today.

That wasn't the case. As I did the day before, I picked up Ben from school, and as directed by my parents, took him to a friend's house so he could be distracted as well, since we didn't have any answers. At this point, family members and close friends were reaching out asking if we needed anything, how they could help, and that they were here for us. That freaked me out – all I wanted to do was go to the hospital and see for myself what was happening. I wanted to go scream at the doctors. How could they not know what was wrong with JM?

They continued to run tests – test after test, there still was no solid update. My dad came home that night and my Mom stayed at the hospital with JM. My dad, Ben, and I had dinner, and got Ben ready for school the next day. At this point, Ben was just as worried as I was.

CHAPTER 16

Locked-In – Trapped in His Body

(Vickie)

When we returned, they moved us to a room down the hall across from the nursing station. I thought it was odd at the time, but they said they were going to put him here so they could more closely watch over him. John Michael was not back from the test yet.

As we walked into his new room, the doctors were there. After a litany of tests, and many speculations, they had finally seen the clot that had formed in John Michael's brain stem. Well, now we had the answer. Our son had suffered a massive brain stem stroke and was experiencing a condition called "locked-in syndrome."

Locked-in syndrome is a medical condition, usually resulting from a stroke, that damages part of the brain stem. When someone is locked-in, the body and most of the facial muscles are paralyzed, but consciousness remains, and the ability to perform certain eye movements is preserved. The doctors explained all of this, then continued by saying John Michael would probably be a quadriplegic for the rest of his life. There was nothing they could do, and this was the worst news we could receive. My brain could not even comprehend what had just been said, and my heart could not accept it. I almost collapsed, turning away in grief and disbelief. I couldn't breathe.

Once the doctors left the room, Mick and I sat down, actually more like collapsed, on the couch in the room. We were in complete shock and disbelief. My only thought was that I needed to call my sisters. I picked up the phone and called my sister closest to me in age. Barely audible, the only thing I could intelligibly get out of my mouth in between sobs was, "You have to come now."

Memories from Vickie's sister, Big Maria

When Vickie called and told us the new MRI had found a blood clot on JM's brain stem and that he had had a stroke, we were devastated. We immediately packed up and headed to the airport. My daughter Casey, drove us. We did not have tickets, but my husband Bill and my sister's friend worked behind the scenes ahead of time, so we could pay and pick up tickets once we got to the airport. It was so sudden that my sister left candles burning in her home. We were a wreck and a sight to behold! We had all been crying and had not bothered to change clothes or look in the mirror. People and security checked us out multiple times!

We landed at the Daytona airport, and because it was midnight, we spent the night there before making the drive to the hospital the next morning. It just did not seem real. We kept hoping that by the time we got to the hospital this would all be over. JM would be better and would be going home soon. We were not prepared for what we were about to see once we arrived in Orlando.

Memories from Vickie's sister, Mercedes

John Michael had a stroke. When LM called and gave us the news, I told my husband Keith that we had to go. He went upstairs as I called my daughter Alyssa to tell her we were going and would pick her up. Keith came down with shoes and said, "Let's go." I shook my head, and said we needed to pack for overnight because I knew we would not be coming back tonight. We cried all the way there feeling so scared for John Michael and Vickie and what might happen.

When we got to the hospital, Vickie just shook and cried. We went in to see John Michael and prayed over him. We begged God to please let him be okay. The neurologist came and took us out into the hallway to explain that John Michael may come out of this, but he did not believe he would walk or talk again. He said there was not much that could be done. Vickie fell to the floor, and we all cried and held her. We were in shock and utter disbelief.

Memories from Vickie's sister, Little Maria

It was around 5:00 p.m. that day I got her call. My other sister, Big Maria, who lived in the house across the street from me, had just come over as she always did to have a happy hour, as I had been so busy that day running around trying to get my house decorated for Christmas and do last minute Christmas shopping. I answered Vickie's call and heard nothing but hysterical uncontrollable sobs. I couldn't understand anything she was saying. As she finally was able to form words and tell me JM's diagnosis, I couldn't believe what she was telling me. How could this be true? How could this have happened to our Jon Jon? I told her I was getting on the next flight. Panic set in as Big Maria and I scrambled to throw our suitcases together. I remember running around the house in circles in a daze.

Because it was the holidays, all direct flights to Orlando were booked, so we had to fly from Raleigh to Daytona and planned to rent a car and make the one-hour drive from there. I barely remember that flight. I had a middle seat and sat between these two strangers that probably wondered what the heck was wrong with me as I sat and sobbed for my nephew and sister to myself the whole flight.

Once in Daytona, we went to the rental car station and were told they were closing and would not have a car available until morning. That poor rental car agent — I put my head on the counter and just sobbed and told her about JM and that we had to get to Orlando as he may not make it through the night. She prayed with Big Maria and me for JM and told me to have faith, that JM was going to make it. I'll never forget that. She was able to get us a car, but we decided to spend the night in Daytona as it was now late, and my other sister Mercedes and her family were able to get to Vickie and were there with her now. It was better if we came early the next morning.

I only slept because of the Ambien I took. Between my jetlag and my worry as to what we would find once we got to Orlando, I don't think I would have slept otherwise.

Desperate to get there, we woke up early and made the drive. I was so anxious to get there, but also so scared. Once we got to the waiting room, they let Vickie know we were there. I was shaking as I saw here come running down the hall. I ran to her as fast as I could. I'll never forget hugging her and telling her I was here for her and would never leave her. She seemed like a zombie, going through the motions but not really knowing what to do. My sister is so very strong, but my heart broke for her as I saw her dealing with what has to be the most horrific news a mother could ever hear about her child.

CHAPTER 17

We Need a Miracle
(Vickie)

It was now Wednesday the 16th. We had kept Ryan and Ben away from the hospital. Our thought was that they would come as soon as he was better so they wouldn't have to see him hooked up to four IVs and all the machines. After learning of his stroke, we called Ryan to come to the hospital. When she arrived and we told her what had happened to her brother, she immediately broke down in tears and fell to her knees. It was a raw moment that I hope to never have to experience with her again, but it did force me to step into "mom mode" and forget my own pain and sadness for a moment in order to comfort her.

When I say that my sisters came now, they came now! I am the youngest of four girls, the Jones girls, as we are often called. My family is originally from Cuba. That said, two of my sisters are named Maria – don't ask! We refer to one as Big Maria and the other as Little Maria. Anyone who grew up with us will refer to them that way as well.

When I made that call to Little Maria, she happened to be with Big Maria. They were in Raleigh, North Carolina and had been on standby for the last couple of days hoping they would not have to come. Of course, they were ready just in case, and they literally closed their suitcases, hopped in the car, and headed for the airport. They could barely speak when they were trying to purchase their plane tickets. The lady behind the ticket counter thought they were crazy. Not many people buy their tickets at the counter these days and not many people show up at the airport in their "comfy clothes" and no makeup looking like they had just been run over by a Mack truck. Plus, they have the same name! So they made it on the plane but had to fly into Daytona and rent a car. Daytona is only an hour away, but they arrived late and were emotionally exhausted, so they decided to get some sleep and drive over first thing in the morning.

Meanwhile, Mercedes, my other sister, immediately jumped in her car with her husband and daughter and drove over from Tampa. Normally it's about a two-hour drive, but they made it in an hour and a half! This is where it all becomes a little foggy for me. Shock had completely set in, and I can only remember fragmented pieces at a time. I remember them arriving and crying and praying, but the details are fuzzy. I remember talking to the pediatric neurosurgeon and not truly understanding a word he said. It is hard to describe it. I was there, but I wasn't. I just remember all I could say to anyone was, "We need a miracle."

Memories from Vickie's sister, Mercedes

Many folks from Winter Park started coming to the hospital in support of John Michael and Vickie and her family. Later that night, Ryan, who was home with Ben, came to the hospital. As she turned the hallway corner and saw us in the hallway outside of John Michael's room, you could see the look of fear and confusion on her face.

So many came in to pray for him, and in hindsight, it was because they didn't expect him to make it. I came to find out much later that we were told that by the doctor, but I honestly don't remember. I think I just I blocked it out. The next thing I remember is my sister taking me home to sleep. Ryan and Mick were going to stay with him that night. This is how I know I was not in my right mind. I would have never left his side for a second if I thought he wasn't going to make it through the night.

Once I arrived home, I was greeted by Ryan's sweet best friend and her sister. They are like family to us. They had been staying with Ben while Ryan went to the hospital. To hear them tell the story of me walking in is surreal. I barely remember. I just remember them trying to make me food because I had not eaten. The next thing I remember is my niece giving me something to help me sleep. I slept in John Michael's bed that night because it made me feel close to him.

Memories from John Michael's sister, Ryan

That next day, it was a Wednesday, we finally had answers. It was after dinner when I received a call from my Mom. I think that was the first time I heard her voice in three days. She said, "JM is awake and he wants to see you." I sobbed. I was relieved and everything was okay and I could finally go see my brother!

My close friends Molly, her sister Rainey and Lauren were over at that time. Lauren offered to drive me to the hospital while Molly and Rainey stayed with Ben. We all were so relieved and believed JM was stable and okay.

As soon as Lauren and I pulled up to the front of the hospital, I saw a family friend Elyse, and it was at that moment I knew everything was not okay.

I hugged her and she looked stoic, not saying anything. I got my badge at the PICU desk, went up the elevator with her, and when I got off the elevator, I saw my Aunt Sadie, Uncle Keith, Alyssa, and Elyse's husband Scott. They looked at me with sadness in their eyes and I just started crying. Where is my mom? Dad? JM? I need to see them. What is going on?

My parents walked out of the PICU hallway and greeted me, both looking like they had been crying for hours and had something terrible to tell me. My mind went to the worst place in that moment: is JM ok? What's happened? I was freaking out, screaming, crying.

I walked back toward JM's room with them when my mom held my hand and said, "JM suffered a brain stem stroke. He is locked-in, which means he can't move or speak."

I couldn't even let her finish before I completely fell to the ground, emotion taking over my entire body I screamed and sobbed to the point where the nurses asked us to go out in the waiting room, that I couldn't do that in there.

I just cried for the next hour. We were all a mess; my parents held my hand as everyone huddled around in the waiting room. They said I had to get it together and calm down before I could go in and see JM. I was scared, nauseated, and shaking, I didn't know what to expect. In your lifetime you may think you'll have to visit a grandparent, hopefully not a parent, but definitely not your younger sibling in a hospital bed.

It really was a blur, but I remember standing outside JM's room for about 10 minutes just looking in, holding my mom's hand and not knowing how I was going to walk in there. I just wanted to hug him and tell him everything was going to be okay. But it was hard and devastating. My first thought was that I needed a

Bible; I needed to pray with him and read him verses. That's how we would find comfort and strength.

I finally walked into his room, and the second I did, I never went back to the scared girl that stood outside the door. I put on my brave face, my strongest self, and decided that's what I was going to be for my brother. He can't see me fall apart; he needs me to be his biggest cheerleader, hopeful and encouraging. He needs me right now, and that above all else was where I wanted to be.

I stayed in the room with JM that night along with my dad. My Aunt Sadie took my mom home. She hadn't been home in three days and desperately needed a good night's sleep. I was forever thankful her sister was there to take care of my mom.

That night was brutal. My dad and I didn't sleep. I think I dozed off for 20 minutes and then woke up to my dad sobbing. He sat on a chair by JM's bed with his head in his hands just absolutely losing it. I quickly sat up and put my arms around him and cried with him. It was a moment I'll never forget. We both just sat there helpless and confused, wanting to believe this had all been a horrible dream.

The next morning, doctors were in and out. I was listening, but reluctant to engage. When my mom returned, she said all her sisters were on the way. I remember going down to get my Aunt Ria and Aunt Mia; they were both running down the hallway in tears. I honestly felt numb. I didn't know what to say to anyone.

I continued to sit by JM. I held his hand and read him Bible verses. He hadn't opened his eyes since I'd seen him. He was on several medications, which just made him sleep. Those next few days were such a blur. Family and friends flooded the waiting room. I remember calling my closest friends, but I don't even remember what I told them. I think I just cried and said things are bad.

JM's neurologist explained what locked-in syndrome was to my family, and it truly is the picture of the perfect nightmare. The blessing in all of it was that JM had full brain function. He was himself 100%. The horrific part was that his brain could not connect to his functions, movement or speech. Of course, we all Googled what this meant, which is never a good idea. Realizing how rare this case is, there were several recovery stories, which we clung onto for hope.

Memories from Ryan's best friend, Molly

I remember driving home from Ole Miss for Christmas break when I got a phone call from Ryan. She sounded anxious and uneasy when she proceeded to tell me that her mom had to pick up JM from school because he was having tunnel vision and was going to the emergency room. I then started to tell her it was going to be okay and that the emergency room was the right place to go because they know what they are doing. She agreed with me, but I knew she was still concerned.

A few hours went by and I got another phone call from Ryan. This time she sounded more distraught. On the phone, Ryan told me the doctors thought JM was suffering from vertigo, but once they gave him the medicine he stopped talking, moving, and responding all together. She told me they were transferring him from Winter Park Hospital to Florida Hospital because they were better equipped there. After hearing this, I was speechless, and I did not know what to say. At first Ryan and I thought maybe JM was allergic to the medicine and his body went into shock. That night, I stayed with Ryan at her house because I wanted to keep her calm and distracted while her parents stayed with JM overnight.

A few days later, I was at dinner with my dad and sisters when I got a text from Ryan asking if I could come over and watch Ben because her parents were finally letting her go see JM. I finished my dinner quickly and headed over to Ryan's house with my sister Rainey. When Rainey and I got there, we were all so excited because we thought JM was better and talking, since her parents were allowing her to see him (Ryan does not handle hospitals or these types of situations well). So I gave Ryan a huge hug, told her I was so happy, and she was out the door.

Ben was in bed, so Rainey and I opened a bottle of wine and started watching TV. A few hours went by before Rainey and I heard the side door open. We both turned our heads very quickly, eager to hear good news because we thought it was Ryan. But it was not Ryan, it was Mrs. Night and her sister, Aunt Sadie.

Looking at Mrs. Night, we immediately knew it was not good news, but stupidly asked how everything was anyway. Now, Mrs. Night is a small, petite, and extremely strong woman, but that night she looked different. She looked frail, weak, and defeated. While walking toward us, her voice cracked and with tears in her eyes said, "It is not good, girls. JM had a stroke."

Immediately, Rainey and I got up to hug Mrs. Night, speechless while she crumbled in our arms. Rainey and I did not know what to do, so we offered to heat her up some food because she looked incredibly exhausted. While she helped us get leftovers out of the fridge, I could see her body shake with fear and concern for her son. It took everything in me to keep it together, not for my sake, but for Mrs. Night's. I did not want her to see me get upset because I did not want to make the situation even worse for her or have her worry about me when all her energy needed to be with JM.

Before Rainey and I finally left their house, Mrs. Night asked me to call Ryan because she wanted to talk to me. I remember walking out of the house through the side door, taking two steps, and bursting out into tears. Looking at my sister crying, we were both without words. My best friend's brother, the brother I never had, had a stroke at 17 years of age. What was I supposed to say to Ryan? Will Mrs. Night be okay?

Seeing Mrs. Night in this state is a sight I will never be able to get out of my head. She is always happy-go-lucky and the-life-of-the-party type of woman. Mrs. Night is the caretaker. She is selfless and puts others before herself. But that night, she was a different Mrs. Night. She was a ghost that I had to take care of. She acted as if she were going through the motions but was outside of her own body. She was numb with fear and exhaustion. Mrs. Night says she does not remember this night, but for me, it was a night I will never forget. This entire experience has changed my life, and I look up to Mrs. Night more than ever before because of her resilience, patience, and extreme strength. I love her!

CHAPTER 18

I Can't Be That Mom

(Vickie)

The next morning, I awoke early and headed to the hospital with my sister. We spoke again with the neurosurgeon. He suggested trying stem cell therapy. They would use John Michael's own bone marrow, spin it, and insert the new cells back into his body intravenously. We agreed, and the procedure would be done the following day. We had nothing to lose, and we had to try anything and everything.

I truly believe, in my heart, that this is why John Michael is able to breathe on his own. For how massive his stroke was and with all the research I have done and people I have spoken with, I have found very few locked-in patients who did not need a tracheotomy. I praise God every day that he did not need it!

Memories from Vickie's sister, Big Maria

When we arrived, we were greeted by lots of Vickie and Mick's friends and our sister, Mercedes, and her family. Everyone looked so sad and stunned. Vickie came out of JM's room and was distraught. She could barely stand, and it was difficult to understand her because she was crying. I was devastated! How could this be happening? She filled us in with the diagnosis and told us some things the doctors had said about his condition. They were not very hopeful, but they did not know John Michael.

I also learned the importance of having an advocate when you are dealing with hospitals and doctors. When the doctors spoke to us, all we could hear was mumbling. It sounded like the teacher from Charlie Brown! It was like we were frozen. I tried to listen, but my brain did not want to hear what was being said. I found that in the middle of this horrific tragedy, I could not read or process much of anything at one time.

Mick and I will be forever grateful to all who stood in the gap for us during this time. We quickly saw just how wonderful our friends are and how great of a community we have. I have seen the love of Christ in how He provided, and still provides for us, through our community. My friendships have deepened as well as my love for my community. I am in awe at the willingness of others, especially those who barely know us, to help in so many ways. It has been humbling, to say the least.

We have said from the beginning that something good has to come from John Michael's stroke. We have seen purpose in our suffering. While it doesn't change our circumstance, it gives us hope and helps us make it through every day.

Ben, who was only ten at the time, came to the hospital on Friday, his last day of school before Christmas break. His cousin, who is his age, arrived as well. The hospital family counselor spoke to them before they saw John Michael to prepare them and help them better understand what had happened. There is no easy way to explain to someone so young that your older brother you look up to is no longer the same.

The days that followed all seemed to run together. I just remember being scolded by doctors and friends to eat, rest, and have a clear mind, because I was no good to my son if I didn't. I would need to be making decisions for him and needed a clear mind. That was easier said than done. I was in shock, shaking and hardly able to speak. I was exhausted, only going home to grab a quick shower.

Every morning and night the team of doctors, nurses, nutritionists, etc., would have meetings for each patient outside of their rooms before going in to check on them. One night I was standing outside of John Michael's room listening in, when I happened to catch a glimpse of myself in the reflection of the door. I thought, "Who is this person?"

I looked as if I had been through a war, which honestly, I felt I had, with no makeup, my hair a mess, and Lord only knows what I was wearing. I remember thinking to myself, *John Michael does not want to see me like this.* So from that day forward, I made sure I not only showered, but put on makeup, did my hair, and wore a cute outfit. I vowed that I was going to make his life as normal as possible, and me looking like death was not going to help him. I was sure he wanted (and needed) to see me as I always was, which was put together. Of course, I realized that I was anything but put together. I just wasn't going to let him see that!

There is no way you can ever prepare yourself for receiving horrific news about your child. How in the world did I become "that mom"? What I mean is, when bad things happened in my life, my motto was always, "At least I'm not that mom sitting by her child's hospital bed." And there I was, *that* mom. Sadly, I am by no means the only one. There are far too many of us. I was thrown into a group I really had no desire to be a part of, ever. But I have met the most amazing women who have inspired me and encouraged me when I did not know which way was up! I feel so blessed to be in this group with them.

CHAPTER 19

Waking Up to Reality
(John Michael)

Ihave so many "first memories" from the PICU that I don't even know which ones are real, much less what order they came in. To be honest with you, a lot of my time there was blocked out of my memory. I can't tell you for sure what happened first, but I remember my mom telling me I had just been visited by some of the guys on the Ponte Vedra lacrosse team. I remember her showing me the trophy they had won that weekend and being upset that I wasn't conscious during the visit.

My room had all kinds of framed pictures of me. I remember thinking I was dying. I never really had that "oh my gosh, what happened" kind of panic moment, which is incredibly strange, considering I could only move my eyes up and down. When I say I could only move my eyes, you need to understand that means zero movement in my head or any of my limbs. I couldn't even open my mouth to command. For some reason, though, I always had this peace about me that I was in God's hands. No matter what this was, He had it under control.

Naturally, I didn't know what day it was when I started "waking up," but I now know that it took the doctors almost three days to find out what happened, at which point it was far too late to do anything about it from a medical/operational standpoint.

TPA is a drug that can help essentially get rid of blood clots and improve blood flow in the brain. It's proven to work best when given within the first three hours of onset of symptoms. We arrived at the ER in under 30 minutes. It could have done absolutely nothing, or it could have dramatically affected the outcome of what was happening. No one knows because I wasn't given that opportunity. No one knew that a 17-year-old athlete was having a massive stroke right in front of their eyes.

For a while, once they found out, no one would tell me exactly what happened, almost as if they were scared to tell me the truth. I remember one particular conversation between my mom and Ryan in which my mom was going to show me a video East Coast Dyes, a lacrosse company, had made for me. In that moment though, they decided against it because they thought it went into too much detail about what happened to me. Funny how I can remember little things like that, but other moments, even days, just don't exist in my memory. I don't remember when or exactly how I found out that I had had a brain stem stroke and was "locked-in," but I just knew this wasn't it. I wasn't going to settle for this. So my focus quickly shifted to getting better. Come to find out, most locked-in patients either don't progress because they are told therapy won't help (which was never an option) or they don't make it. If they do survive this type of stroke, it is often not apparent that they are "there," so the plug is pulled.

According to my mom, this was never the case with me. She always knew I was there. I have various memories of being rolled down the halls in my bed (I wasn't able to sit in a chair) to my MRIs and surgeries. The only real surgery I had was the insertion of the feeding tube and the insertion of the breathing tube (if you want to call it that). They had me on oxygen in the beginning but put the breathing tube in for my four-hour MRI, which is what told them what happened. It was in for a little under a week, and when they took it out, I was miraculously able to breathe on my own. I have no recollection of this, but praise the good Lord, I was one of the very few with this kind of stroke who did not have to be trached.

The feeding tube (peg tube or G-tube) was a completely different story. When I woke up from the surgery, I experienced probably the worst abdominal pain in my life. I can only compare it to having done about 1,000 sit ups and then having a hole puncher go into your stomach. Let's just say that despite being told it would never come out, it was a good day when it did. What followed were two weeks of the limited therapy they offered, a complete takeover of the hospital, and most of all, utter bafflement.

CHAPTER 20

A Pile of Brokenness

(Vickie)

Mick, Ryan, and I began taking turns staying with John Michael at night. We never left his side. I remember as the days went on, we found ourselves tired and getting impatient and short-tempered with each other. We realized that we were each dealing with and processing everything differently, and we were going to have to start showing each other a little grace, because we needed to not only be there for John Michael, but for each other. This would become more difficult as time passed.

My whole life had just come crumbling down, shattered into pieces. It was like an out-of-body experience. I could see it all crumbling down, and as hard as I tried, I couldn't keep everything from falling apart, falling into a million broken pieces. As time has gone on, I have struggled to glue the pieces back together, but eventually they seem to turn into dust and that is all I have left, a pile of brokenness.

As a mother, I always looked at my kids' milestones. I always appreciated every milestone. I was grateful for ten fingers and ten toes – a healthy baby boy! We made it through the toddler phase and elementary school in one piece. John Michael is a risk taker, always gravitating to the edge. If he rode his bike, he would stop at the very edge of the sidewalk just before the street. Cars would slam on their brakes. John Michael never understood why. He would always say, "I was going to stop." If we went on a hike, he would always hike on the very edge of the mountain. I would tell him to come back to the middle, but something always took him right back to the edge. He was never afraid to try anything. Once he made it to his senior year of high school, I considered it another milestone to celebrate. We had made it through middle school and high school with no real issues. He had done well in school and was all set to go off to college to play the sport he loved. But life got in the way and the road took a major detour.

With many locked-in patients, it takes a while for others to realize that they are "still there" mentally and cognitively. For some reason, we always knew John Michael was there. Once again, it was his eyes. His eyes let us know he was very much there. The way he looked at us with those greenish-blue eyes, you could just feel his presence in his gaze. Because they had run an EEG (an electroencephalogram), we knew that cognitively, he was very much there. An EEG measures the brain's activity level. In technical terms, it is a test used to find problems related to electrical activity of the brain. An EEG tracks and records brain wave patterns. Small metal discs with electrodes are placed on the scalp, and then send signals to a computer to record the results. Knowing he was 100% cognitive was a huge blessing. Through all the brain injury therapy we have been through, seeing those who have lost cognitive ability is heart wrenching.

We were also so grateful he was able to breathe on his own. They had inserted a breathing tube for the four-hour MRI. When they went to remove it after the procedure, they felt his breathing was a bit labored, so they left it in. Four days later, it was finally removed. I remember everyone praying so hard that he would be able to breathe on his own so he would not have to be trached. I cannot even describe the joy in the room when he took those first few breaths! The fact that he survived the stroke and was never trached are just a couple of the many miracles we would witness along this journey.

They had him pretty sedated for the first week. Once he came off most of the medication, he was definitely more alert and ready to participate in conversations, which was a good thing, because he would begin to have an influx of visitors.

We stayed in the PICU for three weeks, but it felt like forever. It became our new norm, and everyone became like family. We had the most amazing outpouring of love and support. We had meals delivered to the hospital and to our home every day. Often times we had too much food and would share with other families on the floor as well as the hospital staff. The hashtags #JohnMichaelStrong24 and #JMStrong24 became a trend. The color purple was chosen for hope. People were taking pictures holding up the number 24 and posting it on his Facebook page. John Michael's lacrosse jersey was #24 and it became a symbol of hope as well. There were prayer vigils, a tree dedicated to John Michael in the central park, wristbands, JMStrong t-shirts, bumper stickers, purple ribbons on just about every tree in town, rides and playdates for Ben, cards, notes, texts, and the list goes on and on. I had seen many people rally around and support others who have faced tragedy in our community, but I had never seen anything like this. Our church and school communities were our rock throughout this time. Our church had a prayer service in the chapel. So many attended that they had to move it into the main church! The local news stations had segments on him. His story touched thousands.

A Caring Bridge page and a meal calendar were created for John Michael to keep everyone updated and give opportunities to help. I hated the thought of it. I have been a member of other pages, but I never wanted my own page. Having a page meant there was something horribly wrong. Only people in major tragedies have pages. I didn't want to be this person. It meant I needed help, and I did not want help. I liked to be the one helping. I had no clue how much help I was going to need and how grateful I would be for this page. Along with the Caring Bridge page, they created a JohnMichaelStrong24 Facebook page. Currently, he has over 7,000 followers. God is reaching many through this tragedy and good will come from it!

Memories from John Michael's sister, Ryan

Once JM opened his eyes, we quickly created a communication method via an eye board where he could blink to spell out words and sentences to us. It was brutally slow at first, but once we tried several times, it became our crutch for how to understand JM.

As JM's breathing became stronger, they told us the doctor could try and remove the breathing tube to see if he could breathe on his own. This was huge, the fact that they believed he may not need a trach, that he could breathe independently, would be incredible news. We prayed; we had everyone praying. I remember standing behind his bed wiping the sweat from his hair and rubbing his back, saying over and over, you can do this JM, you can do this.

What we all witnessed in that hospital room was a miracle. God was in that room; it was so obvious and real. I watched JM fight for his breath. I've never seen anyone fight that hard in my entire life. The sweat and determination, there's no other word for it than "miracle." From that moment forward, I think that gave everyone a little bit of hope and transitioned our trust and mindset to believe no matter what the doctors said, this is John Michael we're talking about. He's going to do this. He's going to defy all odds.

CHAPTER 21

The Squad
(Vickie)

The best was the amazing love and support John Michael received from his friends. John Michael has a small close-knit group, "The Squad." I will never forget when they first came to see John Michael. They were at a loss. Their once full-of-life, happy-go-lucky friend was now lying there lifeless. His oldest friend, Rowly, walked into the room, then went straight into the bathroom and cried. But when he came out, he was determined to be the best friend he could be and to help his friend overcome this tragedy. Even his camp friend Connor immediately drove all the way from Myrtle Beach, South Carolina to be with him.

And so it began. Every day this "squad" would show up and make John Michael laugh. They brought in an Xbox and asked if he wanted to go first, which John Michael thought was hilarious. They grabbed Santa hats and brought in a Christmas tree. They even played hide-and-go-seek. At this point we had developed a communication system with John Michael. Big open eyes meant yes and closed eyes meant no. They would turn out the lights and someone would hide. When the lights came back on, they would ask John Michael if the person was hiding under the bed or in the closet or in the bathroom. John Michael would give them a yes or a no with his eyes. They kept it real. They never treated him as if he were any different than he was before. They never spoke down to him, they didn't sugar coat things for him, and they didn't act like life has not gone on. He wants to hear their stories – especially the ones where they are just being crazy boys.

And crazy boys they were. I used to refer to them as Dumb, Dumber, and Dumbest, and they could decide who was who. Growing up with all sisters, I was pretty clueless about raising a boy. They are an eclectic group. The squad was made up of a lacrosse player, a soccer player, two baseball players, and a musician. A few of their many antics included racing to or from school in their cars, jumping off the roof of my house into the pool, sneaking out of the house late at night, and throwing a party in an empty house with no flooring or electricity! They may have been a bit crazy, but they were good boys with big hearts, and at the end of the day, they all had goals and dreams that kept them from taking their antics too far. They are my bonus children. They refer to me as "Momma Noche." They have learned over the years that I will love them, feed them, and have a great time with them, but don't make Momma Noche angry – her Cuban comes out and it is not always pretty. I might be small, but I can be fierce.

All joking aside, they truly have shown tremendous character these last three years. They continue to be here for their friend. I know it means the world to John Michael, and it definitely does to me.

He also had visits from many of his fellow lacrosse teammates and famous athletes as well. Several lacrosse players he has played with throughout the years drove quite a distance to see him. A couple of visits that stand out are one from three players from his Ponte Vedra team. They drove down from Jacksonville to see him and pray over him. Their prayer was so amazing, so mature for boys so young. We were blown away.

A few other players he played with on the Under Armour team also came to visit. Their visit was much lighter. They had him laughing so hard, telling stories of their shenanigans at the tournament. It was the first time he had laughed since his stroke!

Several very special visits included a visit from Brendan Fowler, the face-off specialist for Duke a few years back. He was in town to do a clinic that John Michael was supposed to attend. He was definitely one of John Michael's favorite lacrosse players. He was thrilled to meet him. Brendan continues to stay in touch and has visited John Michael several times.

Anyone who knows our family knows we are huge Florida State fans. John Michael was beyond excited to have Jacques Patrick visit as well as a FaceTime call with Dalvin Cook and Coach Fisher! Gestures like these have helped tremendously in his rehab.

CHAPTER 22

Time to Get to Work
(John Michael)

It felt like we were at the PICU for so much longer than we were. We were there for a total of 21 days. I was given an hour of speech and an hour of PT every day. I don't even remember what we worked on in speech because of how little I could do. My speech therapist was such a sweet lady. She would absolutely kill me for telling this story, but since she won't be named, I think it's okay. Just remember this is in no way a reflection of her as a therapist!

One time, we were working on pursing my lips around a Dum Dum lollipop. I don't remember how, but the round hard candy part was dislodged from the stick and landed in my mouth! We were the only two in the room and I couldn't even open my mouth, much less swallow. I remained relatively calm during the whole thing, I was just thinking, "Here we go." Though probably one of the scariest moments in her life, she managed to pry my mouth open and get it out! That was the last time we worked with lollipops.

In PT, we worked mostly on range of motion. One day, the therapist was holding my leg bent and told me to push it out straight. I was able to tap into my right quad a trace amount! I think that's the first thing I was able to move volitionally (on my own), and it was an amazing feeling not only for me, but everyone in the room. Eventually they started to have me sit up on the edge of the bed. This was no easy feat with 175 pounds of dead weight and no head control. Speaking of which, it's incredible how fast you lose muscle by not doing anything. By the time we left there, I was down easily 20 pounds. What's even more incredible is that, by the grace of God, I kept the muscle tone in my legs. They had no atrophy. Today they look pretty much how they would if this hadn't even happened.

Anyway, the first couple times I went from laying down to sitting up were extremely painful. It felt like all the bones and muscles in my back were stiff and tight. Once in that position, someone held my head and helped me try and move it left, right, up, and down. This exhausted me. Of course, I also wasn't sleeping at night. Imagine your neck is in an uncomfortable position and you can't move it. All I can say is, thank God I was still considered pediatric and someone was allowed to stay with me. There was a nurse coming in to check on me every few hours or so in the night, I remember counting, literally counting the seconds and just praying until he or she came in. I would consider myself a bit more than fairly strong-willed, but honestly, if I was in the regular ICU, I really don't know if I could have done it.

Eventually they had me sit in a chair. Again, this was a difficult task because I had four IVs and had to be hoisted out of bed with a sling and a manual crank. It was not a normal wheelchair. It was a larger, dark blue one with a reclined back. They had to use all kinds of straps to keep me from sliding right out. In the beginning, I could only tolerate a few minutes at most of being out of bed. Again, it felt like we were there a lot longer than we were. I got to the point where I could be rolled down the hall into the visiting area or even to the garden outside the building. I could still only tolerate about 30 minutes to an hour sitting up in a chair.

I would be remiss if I didn't talk about my unbelievably incredible friends. I am blessed with numerous amazing friends but I, of course, am referring to my core group of about six friends from Trinity. One of the first things they did was buy an Xbox for the room. My best friend, Rowly, turned to me and said "Wanna go first?" That's what I'm talking about. They never viewed me differently for a second. I am, and always will be, John Michael to them. No matter what.

My other best friend, Connor, immediately drove nine hours right to the PICU from South Carolina as soon as he heard what happened. They all wore Santa hats and took a Christmas tree from the lobby and brought it up to my room on Christmas Eve. They brought in one of our favorite funny movies, and they know exactly which one I'm talking about. I never told anyone this, but I came to realize that at the time, it actually hurt to laugh. So that was the happiest I'd ever been in pain. More importantly, a distraction from the obvious. I'm not going to tell you the name of the movie, but let's just say it came out in the early 2000s and there are puppets – remember, we are 17-year-old boys!

Everyone massaged my hands and feet which, at times, was comical and sometimes pretty annoying. My mom can probably tell you better just how many people came to visit the hospital. It ranged from almost all across the state and beyond. I'll never forget how the Bannatyne family was there for me. They moved to Maitland in 2011 and Riley, their oldest daughter, is one of my closest friends. She went to Winter Park High School and currently wears number 24 for women's lacrosse at Florida Southern College.

My aunt Mia came all the way from London, where they were living at the time – London! I can't even begin to describe how much of a blessing and help my mom's three sisters were in her time of need. My perspective was limited to the number of people they let back to my room and the few times I made it out to the visiting area. Numerous people came in just to pray over me. From what I've been told, they had more food than they knew what to do with in that hospital, enough to feed the nurses, other patients, and their families and still have some left over.

Early on we found a way for me to communicate with my eyes using a chart comprised of letters arranged alphabetically and split up into numbered rows. One time my best friend Jared and his dad (the school principal and my advisor at the time) were in the room, and I spelled out that I would walk at graduation. It certainly was not how I envisioned at the time, but with the help of my three best friends (Rowly, Jake, and Jared), I did just that.

When we realized that I needed more intensive therapy and I became strong enough to leave, we started to look for an in-patient rehab facility. Come to find out, Orlando doesn't have one for pediatrics. I wasn't 18 for another three months, so our options were Brooks in Jacksonville or the Shepherd Center in Atlanta. I remember this was a heavily debated decision even just from my perspective in the room. We eventually decided on going to the Shepherd Center. We didn't know how long we would be there.

When my dad showed me the video for the Shepherd Center, I got emotional. Seeing people in wheelchairs learning to walk again just made it all real. Here I was a few weeks ago, arguably the best face-off midfielder in the state, and now what? But I quickly learned that lacrosse did not define me. You can take away everything, but you can't take away my identity. You can find that at the cross. God did not bring me this far to leave me here. Only He can get me back to where I want to be and I will trust in Him.

CHAPTER 23

Learning to Communicate
(Vickie)

The fact that John Michael survived is nothing short of a miracle! His stroke was massive and completely knocked out every connection from his brain to his body. It took me almost two years to truly realize this. Over those three weeks, we learned what locked-in really meant. We quickly learned not to Google things. There was not much on the internet that gave us hope. "Locked-in syndrome affects around 1% of people who have a stroke. It is a condition for which there is no treatment or cure, and it is extremely rare for patients to recover any significant motor functions. About 90% die within four months of its onset." Well, that's not very positive, now is it?

We did, however, find a couple of stories of others who had overcome locked-in syndrome, and this is where we started. The first thing we did was develop a communication system that our good friend, Scott, and major advocate with the doctors, found. It is a letter chart. There were five rows. The first row consisted of the vowels. The next four rows were the rest of the alphabet in order. When John Michael wanted to say something, we would start with the first letter of the first word. We would ask, "Is it in Row 1, Row 2, Row 3, Row 4 or Row 5?" He would give us a yes with his eyes. So if he was spelling "mom," he would have given a yes for Row 3, because M is in Row 3. For the O, he would give a yes for Row 1 and another yes for Row 3 for the last M. It took a while to get it down, but by the time we arrived at the rehab facility, we had it memorized. Actually, Ben had it memorized first, and that motivated the rest of us to do so as well. We all became very good with this system, so much so that people were amazed at how quickly we could spell sentences.

You would think someone from John Michael's generation would have communicated like they do when they text, but not John Michael. He was spelling full sentences and using correct grammar and an extensive vocabulary. He always kept us on our toes. He would always ask please and say thank you. I was so happy I taught him good manners, but there were days when I was thinking, "Really? Can't you just say 'scratch nose' instead of 'Can you please scratch my nose?'" We used a dry erase board at first to write down each letter until we became so proficient we could do it in our heads. He spelled out many humorous things for us as well as some pretty heart wrenching thoughts. One of the hardest was "I will not play my senior year." Oh, if we had only realized at the time that that would be the first of many things he would miss out on.

CHAPTER 24

Christmas Celebration

(Vickie)

While we were in the PICU, Christmas came. When I say I have incredible friends, this is no overstatement. They finished my shopping and bought more for my kids than I would have! Meals were prepared and everything was beautiful – except John Michael was not there.

I did not want to celebrate Christmas. If I could have, I would've had everything boxed up and put back in storage. I hated everything about it – the songs, the festive decorations, the joyful people. I wished it all away. But thanks to my sisters and their families, we did celebrate Christmas. For the first time maybe ever, I celebrated Christmas for the right reason. You see, without the birth of Jesus, I would have no savior, and oh, how I needed a savior. For the first time, I honestly did not care about one gift or how my house looked. I did not obsess if everything was perfect. I just knew I needed Jesus more than ever.

Our friend Elyse stayed with John Michael Christmas Eve so Mick and I could be at home. The next morning, after we opened gifts, we headed to the hospital. We brought John Michel's presents, but I insisted we leave them in the car. I thought there was no way he was going to want us to open his gifts. Well, I was wrong! He was very excited about them. Later that morning, Christmas carolers came singing and walking into each patient's room. I thought, "Close the doors! John Michael is not in the mood for Christmas songs." Again, I was wrong. He wanted the doors open and wanted to hear the music. He welcomed the music. He obviously needed Jesus too!

Memories from Vickie's sister, Little Maria

In those early days, Vickie was often shaking uncontrollably and making guttural noises I am sure she wasn't even aware she was making. I wanted so badly to fix things for her, but I didn't know how. There were so many decisions to be made and so many people trying to give their opinions. I am sure this added to her stress.

We decided to focus on making the most out of Christmas not only for her and JM but for Ryan and Ben and Mick. So I sent my girls to go shop and buy gifts and food and anything they could think of to salvage Christmas and bring a little hope to us all.

We did celebrate Christmas that year, thankful that JM did make it through the night, thankful that he wasn't trached, thankful he could breathe on his own, thankful his mind was intact and that he was with us. We took turns sleeping in the PICU to try and give Vickie a break, as my super-strong sister now seemed so fragile. Understandably, she did not want to leave JM's side. After the holidays, we eventually all had to leave to go back home. It was so hard saying goodbye. The weight of uncertainty hung heavy on all of us. As traumatic and painful as this sudden rush of bad news had been on all of us, leaving triggered an entirely different set of emotions. Now we were faced with this heavy burden of uncertainty and all of the questions that came along with it.

Would JM recover? Would he be able to speak? The answer according to the doctors was a resounding no. But this isn't what we saw from Vickie. Her faith and resilience are so strong. She didn't believe that for one second.

While we were all lamenting amongst ourselves about what the future looked like for JM, Vickie and her family, Vickie believed he was going to get better, he was going to beat this. What we couldn't see that day, but has become obviously apparent since, there are no two people better prepared to handle this terrible twist of fate than Vickie and John Michael.

So while it is a tragedy that JM spent so much time and worked so hard at lacrosse to be the best and to get that D1 scholarship, it wasn't in vain. Thank God for his discipline, thank God for his determination, thank God for his competitiveness. This is what we are seeing today – his "never give up," his "you aren't going to beat me" attitude. And this is why I know he is going to beat this.

CHAPTER 25

Believe

(Vickie)

Everyone in the PICU became our family. When you spend time on a pediatric ICU floor, you quickly realize you are not alone. There are unfortunately way too many parents sitting by their child's bed praying for a miracle. While we were there, we experienced a family losing a child, a child almost overdosing on their mom's medication, and another stroke patient who was only three years old who had been there since October. There are no words to describe it.

The precious little girl next door to John Michael was the three-year-old. Her sweet mom noticed me, and to this day, I am still amazed and humbled that even though she was living her own nightmare, she thought of me. She went to the gift shop and bought me a sweet bracelet that said "Believe." That bracelet meant the world to me. I don't think I took it off for almost a year.

John Michael was almost six feet tall and 175 pounds! I feel blessed that he was still considered pediatric. He received individual attention and care. He was monitored around the clock.

They started limited therapy with him about a week into our time there. He started speech, occupational, and physical therapy. He loved the speech therapist. She gave him apple juice on a sponge and let him suck on lollipops – which we were later told she should not have done. I am glad she did because it made John Michael happy and obviously it didn't hurt him. At this point he was on a feeding tube and was appreciating a taste of anything.

In physical and occupational therapy, they got him sitting on the edge of the bed with assistance. They actually got him out of bed and into a wheelchair so we could take him outside for some fresh air. This was definitely one of those times where living in Florida in December is a wonderful thing! The fresh air and the cool (but by no means cold) temperature boosted all our spirits.

CHAPTER 26

The Good Shepherd

(Vickie)

We now had the challenge of discussing where we should go from here. He was no longer in critical condition and was ready to get out of the PICU and into a rehab facility. Well, wouldn't you know it, Orlando did not have a pediatric inpatient rehab facility. We would have to find one elsewhere. After much research and many phone calls, we chose to go to The Shepherd Center in Atlanta, Georgia. The saying "It's a Small World" came oh, so true for us.

In our search for the right facility, we quickly learned how many connections we had to the Shepherd Center that we did not even know we had. We were truly one degree separated from the Shepherds themselves! Alana Shepherd actually came by John Michael's room at the center to say hello. As with so much on this crazy journey, we were grateful for the help in getting us in so quickly. Due to the holidays and the New Year, we had to wait until January 5th to be transported. They flew John Michael, Mick, and me up in a medical jet. Mick's brother Brad was so gracious to drive my car to Atlanta while my sister Big Maria stayed behind with Ben. She ended up being at my home taking care of Ben for three months. I will forever be grateful to her for the sacrifice she made to help me. I had such peace knowing Ben would be well taken care of.

When the day came to leave, it was quite the send-off. The day before we left, the chaplain from his school who had visited frequently asked John Michael, "John Michael, we have been praying for you to recover, but what would you like us to pray for?" John Michael spelled out "patience." He must have known better than I did that the road ahead would be long.

Saying goodbye to our friends, family, and everyone on the PICU floor was tough. We had gotten into such a comfortable routine and knew everyone and knew what to expect. The outpouring of family, friends, food, and love got us through those three weeks. I did not realize how much we were going to miss it until we landed on that cold, dreary day in Atlanta.

CHAPTER 27

Where is God?

(Vickie)

It was Tuesday, January 5th. I'm not sure what I expected, but what we walked into did not even remotely resemble anything close to what I was thinking. The small medical jet had landed about 30 minutes from the Shepherd Center. I had been a little panicked during the flight because the altitude had labored John Michael's breathing and they had to give him some oxygen. Fortunately, once we landed, his breathing returned to normal. John Michael and I were transported in an ambulance while Mick rode in an SUV with the transportation company to the center. It was drizzling outside, and for this Florida girl it was freezing – probably 50 degrees!

As we walked in, we were greeted by a lovely lady who would be our case manager while we were there. I could not tell you one word she said. As I looked around and took it all in, all I saw were wheelchairs. Wait a minute – we came here to get better, to get out of a chair. That sinking feeling started creeping back in, the same one I had when the doctors explained what had happened. I had to catch my breath. I kept telling myself to focus, pay attention, and don't let that feeling carry you away.

As we made our way to John Michael's room, I was terrified. Wheelchairs were everywhere – some were going so fast, some I could not even figure out how they were moving because the person driving did not even look like they could move! Patients were "parked" in their wheelchairs in front of the nurse's station looking like they would never make it! I felt as if I had been punched in the gut all over again. I had to remember to breathe. I'm sure I walked around for at least the first month looking like a deer in the headlights. We were no longer in my safe little bubble with all of my friends and family and a whole community waiting and wanting to help. We were alone and scared to death.

Walking into John Michael's room I thought, "Okay, God is so good." John Michael had a corner room, which meant it was a little larger than most and it had a lot of windows. I tend to be a bit claustrophobic, so I was very happy to have that natural light. The walls were empty and white, very cold and stark.

We were first met by his team of doctors, then by his therapists. Again, I could not tell you one word they said. I just remember being told they would start therapy the next day with a complete evaluation. Next, our case manager took us over to see the apartment that was provided for 30 days.

If I'm being honest, I was never comfortable there. It was nothing like home, and even though the apartment was right next door and connected to the Shepherd Center, it seemed like the walk over and back took forever. But mostly, it really bothered me that everything was wheelchair accessible. I thought, "Why on earth are they pushing this whole wheelchair thing? Why aren't they getting people out of their chairs?" I was so naive and clueless as to what the Shepherd Center was all about. I truly believed John Michael would walk out of that facility. I'm not sure if this was from my faith, my hope, my denial, or even my ignorance as to how massive the stroke was and how much damage it caused. It would actually take me a couple of years to accept this.

Our walk over to the apartment was the first time we left John Michael alone without a family member or friend. I was very nervous about this. We had to walk through the parking garage to get to the elevators for the apartments. I kept thinking, "Why is it so cold?" I did not pack appropriately, and I was going to need warmer clothes. When we returned to John Michael's room, we realized we had not eaten all day and it was mid-afternoon. Luckily the center is on a main street with many food options. Mick walked over to Chick-fil-a to grab us a sandwich. This began the many days of late lunches or no lunch at all, since I would not leave John Michael alone.

The plan was that I would spend most of the time there and Mick would trade off so I could go home for a break and be home with Ben. Some weekends, Ben and Mick would both come so we could all be together. It was hard juggling everyone's schedules, but we made it work.

A few hours later Mick's brother arrived with my car and our clothes. They went to the store to get miscellaneous items for the apartment and some food to make our stay there more comfortable. Mick bought more than necessary but made it as much like home as possible. That night they went to dinner while I waited with John Michael for them to bring me something to eat as well. They took forever! By the time they got back and I ate, it was pushing 9:00. I was so emotionally and physically drained at this point. I ate, showered, then headed over to spend the night in John Michael's room.

I was so angry. I thought, "This is not a vacation. Who has time or even wants a leisurely dinner?" I'm sure a lot of that anger was more about what had happened to John Michael and everything that I had experienced up to that point. Sitting in the stark room alone with my son whose life had just been severely damaged gave me too much time to reflect on all that had just transpired in the previous weeks. It was too much, and

I felt like the weight of the world was on my shoulders and I was all alone. Besides dealing with the situation at hand, I had to learn to deal with the fact that Mick and I were not going to handle this in even remotely the same way. This would take an act of God as well.

The chair next to John Michael's bed folded out into a makeshift bed. No, it was not comfortable. We eventually bought a thin air mattress to lay on top of the chair. It helped, but I think I have permanent back damage from it. That first night seemed to last forever. I will never forget it for as long as I live. Once the lights were out, the man in the room next door, who slept in a bed with a safety tent on top, started screaming, "Fire! Fire! Somebody help me! Get me out of here!"

To say I was scared is putting it mildly. We came to learn that he was a military man who was suffering from PTSD. I remember texting my sisters crying and saying, "I can't do this." I was not capable of this. I just lay there in tears, crying and praying for the strength to make it through. Where was God? I felt so alone and abandoned.

It took me a while to be able to answer this question, but as I look back, He was everywhere. Just then, the night nurse came in. He was my guardian angel. If you have ever seen the movie "It's a Wonderful Life," he was my Clarence. Stan was his name. He was the nicest, most godly man. He eased my fears and made us feel comfortable in our new surroundings. I looked forward to the nights when Stan would be taking care of John Michael. We became friends, and just like everyone else who was meeting John Michael for the first time, he loved him. To this day, I find it fascinating that John Michael has not verbally spoken to the people we have met since his stroke, and yet they have all come to love him, love his spirit and determination. It truly is amazing.

I did not wake up rested, but I did wake up excited for John Michael to start his therapy. We needed to get going so John Michael could get better and we could go home. That first day would only be evaluations of what he could and could not do. It was both promising as well as a huge wake-up call as to how far he had to go.

He loved all of his therapists. They quickly learned how to communicate with him and became his friends. Communicating was more important to him than anything. John Michael was to receive speech therapy, physical therapy, occupational therapy, and recreational therapy. I did not have a clue what recreational therapy was all about or why he was "wasting that time." I learned over our time there that recreational therapy was every bit as important as the others. While his other therapies worked on movement and function, recreational therapy taught him how to accept his current situation and integrate back into society.

CHAPTER 28

And So It Began

(John Michael)

Where do I even begin? To be honest with you, a lot of this I don't remember, not because I blocked it out or anything, but because time has passed and so much has happened. I really went into the Shepherd Center with the idea that I was walking out of there. I definitely did not realize how massive the stroke was. Early on my mom was contacted by a woman, Clodagh Dunlop, and I made the mistake of comparing myself to her. I think we all did. Clodagh was from Ireland and also had a brain stem stroke and was locked-in. She, however, was able to walk out of her facility with some assistance after months of therapy. I would soon learn that no two strokes are ever alike.

Since I couldn't tolerate being in a car, much less sitting up for that long (almost seven hours from Orlando), my parents and I were transported to the Shepherd Center in a small

...p, I needed oxygen because of the ..., my mom and I were taken in an ... on the gurney) about 30 minutes ... the Center felt so empty and grim ...rner room with two large windows ... As they tore off the bandages from ...ed me to change into their hospital ...ntle nurses in the PICU. This began ... long and frightful journey of worrying about rolling over or having the G-tube pulled on. Most of the time I wore a binder around my stomach to prevent this from happening, but it still did. Imagine there is a tiny golf ball inside your stomach and it's attached to a string coming out the other side. Now imagine someone tugs the string, even lightly. Not fun.

At the Shepherd Center, the focus was on intense therapy. They started me out on a tilt table just trying to get me to bear some of my weight. They incrementally raised me up onto my feet. Someone would have to stand on something next to the table and hold my head up to keep it from falling forward or to the side. I wore a blood pressure cuff to make sure my BP didn't drop too low after not having been upright in almost a month. If it dropped, they would just lower the angle back down and wait until it normalized to start again. It would be a little while before I was able to get to a 90-degree angle. It's also crazy how self-aware my body became. Whenever my blood pressure did get too low, I became sweaty and itchy. What would you do if you had an itch you couldn't scratch? Yeah, I don't know either.

I remember one distinct time at Shepherd trying to spell out "itch." I got to "I-T…" and they assumed the word was "it," so naturally when I spelled "C-H" it did not make any sense. After several minutes of struggling to understand, this person began to get upset (mostly with themselves, I'm sure) which just made me upset and the whole process harder. All the while my body was screaming out and in agony. Eventually I had to just let it go and deal with it until it subsided, which I unfortunately have had to become somewhat accustomed to. That's what I get for trying to be polite.

My mom tells stories from in the beginning (if it was something less urgent) where I would literally say, "Can you please… " Note to self: just say "scratch."

This would only be the start of my spelling woes. While at Shepherd, we hired a lovely woman named Carla to stay with me at night so my mom could get some rest. I was her "baby boy." No young man should have to endure all the coddling I've dealt with, but regardless, it was sweet. Anyway, one night I woke up and my pillow was bothering me. I simply wanted it readjusted.

I got her attention and began to spell, "P-I-L-L… " She stopped spelling; this was unfortunately a common occurrence if someone reached a word within a word. It's not like the word board had a space button, so unless it occurred to someone to ask me if it was the next word then they were really just guessing. Granted, it's the middle of the night and this person is still fairly new to me. She thought I wanted some kind of pill, so she kept asking me about a pill. It was also relatively early on, and I don't think I could shake my head at this point, so I'm lying there closing my eyes as hard as I can beginning to get frustrated.

Another thing you need to know is that I'm completely against medication. At one point, I actually spelled out "no more meds" to my physician at the Shepherd Center. In any case, Carla and I were getting nowhere so she called in one of the nurses to help. Now I was really upset. We were making this whole scene in the middle of the night over nothing, a misunderstanding. I wanted my pillow moved a few inches under my arm. Eventually (I think) they realized I wasn't talking about a pill, but they never figured it out, so I just let it go.

Don't even get me started on trying to make words plural or the word "an." God only knows how many times I've had to spell the same word over and over. "You just said that!" People would exclaim until they realized there was an "s" at the end of the word. "OMG. Really, JM?" they would say jokingly. IT MATTERS!

Then there's the word "an." People would just assume I was saying "a" and start the next word with "n." So it never made sense. What didn't make sense to me was why people felt the need to speak up when talking to me. The stroke didn't affect my hearing! That's probably my biggest pet peeve, between that and people (sometimes subconsciously) belittling or doubting my comprehension or sensation. I've ALWAYS (thank God) completely had both! I get it. I'm in a wheelchair and can't communicate normally right now but that doesn't mean you should treat me differently... This rarely ever happens anymore but still it's something I've had to deal with.

People also don't think about the fact that not everything is a yes or no question! Especially when it's natural technically to ask a double sided or negative opinion. (For example "this or that" or "are you not..."). It never occurred to me how important the words "I don't know, maybe, and sometimes" are either!

Anyway, another thing we worked on was sitting at the edge of a mat. I hated this exercise in the beginning because I was genuinely terrified I would fall off. They had electric Hoyers there, which greatly simplified the process of transferring me. In the beginning, that was the *only* way to transfer me. There always had to be two people, though, one holding my legs and one holding my head. Eventually, once I had better head control, I was able to sit independently for minutes at a time. In hindsight, I was using a lot of "tone" to do so. I was slouched over, kind of hanging back on my pelvis with my legs kicked out straight. Nonetheless, I started doing this in March. I know that because I remember spelling out, "I will sit up in March." My mom told me I should be proud of myself for saying that. Of course, what she didn't know was that I meant I would sit completely straight up from lying supine in my bed – another example that I had no clue just what exactly had happened. I always set larger than life goals for myself.

If we got there in January and I was sitting independently in March, then I must have begun controlling my head some-time in February. I remember the first time they were able to transfer me in the Hoyer net with just one person and no one holding my head. It was my first glimpse at independence. I attribute my head control largely to the act of lying prone (on my stomach) on a wedge and looking up, left, and right. In the beginning, I hated this exercise as well, mostly because of the pressure it placed on the G-tube, even with the binder. You could never be too sure about how secure it was or if it had gotten loose, so rolling over was always an adventure.

Ali, my PT, was simply just a little woman, smaller than my mom. Once I was able, she would always do standing transfers with me. Somehow, she managed to move me by herself, too. When I had PT first thing in the morning, my nurse Edith would come scurrying into the room, flip on the lights and say,

"Come on, mommas, Ali is waiting!" She also liked to call me John Michaels... a lot.

At first, I was uncertain of how I felt about Edith. "She makes you do everything!" I told my mom. I quickly learned the importance of everything Edith was teaching my mom, and she became one of my favorite nurses. Margaret, Stan, Keita, Susan, Sam, Aisha, and Yolanda were some other favorites, to name a few.

My ST, Alexis, had her hands full. We worked first and foremost on swallowing. She started by giving me ice chips and then thickened liquids (yes, thickened, that's a thing) on a spoon. There is no other way to describe the thickener other than just nasty. I had a couple of swallow studies there which were basically live X-rays of my throat to make sure everything was going down the right way. They mixed everything with barium (this chalky white stuff, also nasty) before I swallowed it so the liquid would show up more easily in the X-ray. I finally passed on my third swallow test, clearing me for thickened liquids and soft puréed foods. I passed about a week after I started using the vital stim (facial stimulation). Aside from pudding and applesauce, my first meal was mashed potatoes and gravy. Hospital food never tasted so good. We were so excited that I finally got a food tray like all the other patients.

Then there was Elliott. Elliott was a therapy tech who, although about six years older, was the closest in age with similar traits as me. Add that up and it's an instant recipe for friendship. He turned 24 while I was there (a little after I turned 18) and as a joke, I had my parents get him a bottle of tequila! My parents paid him to do extra stretching at the end of the day, and I would always try to kick him off the table. Needless to say, we had more than a few laughs. I can promise you I was not laughing when I was getting a shot in my stomach every night for almost 5 months at the beginning of 2016. That's right, every single night before bed at the Shepherd Center (minus the last few days or so) I received a nice Lovenox shot right to the gut. It's basically just an extra blood thinner, probably precautionary, but looking back and knowing how all this happened I'm glad I was on it. It really wasn't all that bad but certainly not how I preferred being tucked in.

I had innumerable different chairs during my stay there. My first real taste of independence came when they put me in a powered wheelchair. It had a button that I could reach with my head. When I pressed and held it, it tilted my chair one way. When I let go, it stopped, and then when I pressed and held it again, it tilted the other direction. I was in control of my position.

Next came driving. There was the sip and puff option which I immediately ixnayed, not only because I couldn't do it at the time, but I thought it looked ridiculous. Then there was a small joystick that wrapped around in front of my face that I controlled with my chin. Yes, I was using my chin to drive the wheelchair. This worked okay, but it wore down my chin. It also wouldn't stay in place for more than 5 minutes, especially when I wanted to move it out of the way. Realistically, I wasn't going to sit there with something in front of my face 24/7.

Finally came the head controls. I don't know why we didn't just start with this; it was almost too easy. Once again, I was learning about patience.

CHAPTER 29

The First Outing

(Vickie)

We had only been at Shepherd for a little over a week when John Michael had his first outing with recreational therapy. In preparation for this outing, the recreational therapist took us across the street to the CVS. I will not lie; I was scared to death. It was a lot of work and a lot of maneuvering. How in the world would I ever be able to do this on my own?

On the first group outing they were taking a group of patients to The College Football Hall of Fame. He was very excited to go. I, on the other hand, was not comfortable with this. I was thinking, "There is no way he is going out in public like *that*." As the day drew closer, I was sure he would back out.

Well, wouldn't you know? He went. I was not allowed to go with him. I was like a mom dropping her toddler off at preschool for the first time. I was a nervous wreck the whole time. I went for a run, took a shower and waited. I think I was nervous mostly because he could not talk to anyone. When I saw the van pull back in, I was so excited. I had not been that excited for weeks. When he got back to his room, I had never been so happy to see him.

He had a good time for the first time in weeks. He even made a new friend with a boy on the spinal injury floor. It was just like John Michael to make a friend and he couldn't even communicate with him. It was easy for him as long as people asked yes or no questions. And again, his eyes would let you know he was engaged and understanding the conversation. If the conversation touched on something that meant something to him or brought up an emotion, his face would light up. The only negative that day was that they took a little break for lunch and they all ate Chick-fil-a in front of him. They obviously weren't thinking. He had not had real food in over a month and that was one of his favorites. Well, of course mom instinct kicked in, and needless to say, they would not be eating in front of him again.

It was all a very humbling experience for me, the first of many. Here I was thinking he didn't want people to see him like "that" – in a chair, unable to speak or move. What will they think? How dare they judge him? If only they knew that he was really this strong, articulate, athletic boy! I couldn't have been more wrong. He did not see himself like that at all.

It was my insecurity that was tested. If I'm being honest, I was always uncomfortable around wheelchairs and the people in them. I assumed. I judged. It was shallow. I'm not sure why I had this fear, but I did. I have overcome many fears throughout these last few years. We had come to Shepherd to change our situation, but what was changed was me. I arrived sheltered and fearful but would leave confident and a much better person having met some amazing people.

CHAPTER 30

The Look of a Warrior

(Vickie)

While John Michael suffered a brain injury, his brain is fine. He is 100% cognitive. Before we had arrived they struggled with where to place him, the brain injury floor or the spinal injury floor. Since a stroke is a brain injury, they chose the brain injury floor. After a couple of weeks, his speech therapist placed a large note behind his bed that said something like "I am 100% cognitive but am unable to speak. Please give me a chance to respond." Many people did not bother to read the sign. One nurse actually came in one night and asked John Michael a series of questions. Questions like, "Do you know where you are? Are you at a hospital? Are you in a hotel?"

John Michael, of course, just laughed at her. We both thought, "No, we are at the Ritz Carlton!" Another morning, someone asked him if he knew what day it was and when he responded with the correct date, she said he was wrong. He corrected her, of course. He was on top of everything. He knew what medication he was taking better than I did. He had to correct a nurse one night who read off the wrong list of meds. Fortunately, they have to scan his wrist band before administering medication, and it would have shown she had the wrong meds. It was a bad comedy show. Again, we had to laugh, otherwise we'd cry.

We saw many horrific things there. The boy two doors down was shot twice in the head by his friend's uncle. The boy four doors down was hit by a car going 45 miles an hour. The boy around the corner suffered a massive brain bleed. The sweet girl next door was hit by a car stepping off of a curb, and eventually another precious young mother arrived who was locked-in as well. The sad stories could go on and on. It was interesting how the majority of patients we encountered there were boys, though.

Like I have said before, just when you think your situation is unbearable, there is always someone else who has it worse. All I had to do was walk out into the hallway. One boy there was making great physical progress, but he had severe brain damage. His mother told me how they would have conversations, and he would not even know she was his mother. This just broke my heart. So while I was envious that he could talk and walk, he had different challenges. The communication system we had may have appeared crazy and tedious, but at least my son knew who I was. I can't imagine how tough that must have been for her. The parents or loved ones, on that floor, we were all the same. We had "that look"–the look of exhaustion, the look of despair while trying to remain hopeful, the look of a warrior who would never give up.

Chapter 31

Healing and Miracles

(Vickie)

During that first week, we had a meeting with the doctor. She was a physiatrist. I had never heard of that title before, but she came highly recommended. She would oversee John Michael's health and prescribe medication as needed.

What I am about to say in no way discredits her medical knowledge or ability to care for her patients, but the meeting we had was one of the many horrific moments we would encounter. We had barely been there for a week and had only received limited therapy due to the weekend and the first day being evaluations. I will never forget her words. She basically had the same attitude as the PICU doctor. All I could hear was "your son will never." He will never get off the feeding tube. He will never speak again. He will never get out of that chair, and if we didn't have the means to have private care he would need to be in a facility.

Are you kidding me?

Now don't get me wrong, I do not want anyone to sugar coat anything for me, but not to give even a glimmer of hope was beyond excusable. I just sat there with tears streaming down my face rebuking her in Jesus's name. I refused to believe the horrible things she was saying. I was so grateful that John Michael was not a part of that meeting. I know she could not give us false hope, but to offer no hope was not acceptable.

My initial thoughts were that first of all, you do not know my son and secondly, you could not possibly know my God. My son is an athlete, a fighter, a never-give-up kind of person, and my God is a God of hope, healing, and miracles. I refused to accept what she had to say. I know she was just trying to protect herself and the Center and to help us, but with no disrespect, doctors and science do not have all of the answers. On this journey, I have met and spoken with many people who were given no hope by their doctors. What a horrible shame. The best part is, so many have proven them wrong. John Michael already has and continues to do so!

CHAPTER 32

Waiting, Waiting, Waiting

(Vickie)

We stayed at the Shepherd Center for a little over five months. It felt like we were there for so much longer, but in hindsight it was a blip on the radar. So much happened during those months: the white walls slowly began to fill with posters, cards, pictures, and jerseys. He received so many jerseys, all with the number 24, for him. By the time we left, there was not an empty spot in the room, and there were boxes of items at the apartment. At least once a week we received a stack of cards, gift cards, and care packages, usually from strangers who had heard of his story and wanted to do something to help. I'll never forget how one family who knew my sister actually sent Ben a care package. They had a little boy about the same age. He wrote a sweet note saying he thought Ben might be sad about his brother and hoped the toy and candy would cheer him up. It was so thoughtful and of course, Ben was thrilled for the gift, but also that someone thought of him.

We lived and breathed by "the schedule." By the nurse's station there was a large dry erase board on the wall. On this board they posted the therapies and activities for each patient on that floor that day. I never knew until the night before, or first thing in the morning, when John Michael's therapies would begin and end. Each day he was to have an hour of each therapy. If we were lucky, some days he would get a little extra. Every morning I texted Mick and Ryan to let them know his schedule. If they couldn't be there, they wanted to know exactly what he was doing and when. I learned that OOB stood for "out of bed" and BTB was "back to bed." That board was our life. It was all we had to look forward to on most days.

They once came in around 2:00 in the morning to bathe him. I was amazed and angered. What teenage boy takes a shower that early? I think when they were going to be short-handed in the morning, they must have had to shower patients when they had enough manpower to do so. I would have none of that. John Michael needed his rest as much as he needed therapy, and he would not be showered in the middle of the night. That said, there were days when they were shorthanded and I had to help shower him if I wanted him to have a shower in the morning. This took some getting used to on both of our parts. No 17-year-old wants their mother helping with their shower, nor does any mother want to help shower their 17-year-old child.

Each morning I woke up to someone coming in to take his vitals, and I would step out in the hall and check the schedule board. Within the hour they would be back to shower John Michael and get him dressed for the day. I always prayed they would not need my help. Toward the end, they just assumed I would help so they would only send one person in. However, on the mornings I did not have to help, I grabbed a coffee and a bagel. I typically only had 30 minutes before they finished. I was grateful there was an Au Bon Pain attached to the Center because I did not have time to go to the apartment.

Once I got back, the waiting began. And did we ever wait. Half of our time there was spent waiting – waiting for the therapist to come get him, waiting for a nurse to help him, waiting to talk to the doctor, waiting for friends and family to visit, waiting to go home, waiting for a miracle... waiting, waiting, waiting! In our waiting we learned so much. Patience hasn't been our only lesson. We also learned to let go of our desire to control so much of our lives. We learned to trust – trust in the system at Shepherd even when it didn't always make sense, trust in strangers bringing us meals and giving rides to and from the airport, and most importantly, trust God and His perfect timing. We were told over and over again that this would be a marathon and not a sprint. Well, for this runner, sprinting is what I do. To sit and wait was excruciating. The TV was our only escape, and we didn't even really like watching TV. His high school lacrosse team collected DVDs and brought them to Shepherd. We had almost 200 to choose from. Mick bought a flat screen TV with a built-in DVD player and an Apple TV. It was quite the set-up, and John Michael and anyone who spent time with him greatly appreciated it! It would have been an even longer five months if we had not had it.

CHAPTER 33

Building a New Community
(Vickie)

We began to settle into a routine and once again found a new kind of normal. We truly did come to love everyone there, even the doctor who did not give much hope. I stayed with John Michael most of the time, going home occasionally for a break and to be with Ben. Ryan was in her last semester of college and came on the weekends when she could. When I say John Michael had visitors, that is a complete understatement. I quickly gained a new community of friends in the Atlanta area, some old, some new.

Meals were scheduled for me and rides to and from the airport for friends and family. I would never leave John Michael alone. He could not communicate with everyone, and he had no way to call for help if he needed it. Some days when I was there alone with John Michael, I had no idea how I was going to get lunch or dinner. But God always provided. My sweet friends and sorority sisters randomly stopped by with food for me, some of whom I had not seen since we graduated college! They never knew how much I needed it or how the timing was always perfect. Most called or texted to ask if they could bring something by, but several times, Lynne or Cara would just stop by with a bag full of healthy food. They sometimes just left it at the front desk, knowing I was probably busy with John Michael.

For at least the first two months, almost every day we had someone knock on the door to John Michael's room wanting to meet him, offer him hope, or offer me help. It truly was amazing as well as humbling to have so many care so much. Complete strangers as well as friends took the time to truly live out the gospel – helping others, loving others, and serving those in need. As I've said, I have learned many lessons on this journey.

One of the biggest was learning to receive. I am a giver by nature. I'd rather serve than be served, and I am probably the worst in asking for help. But here I was, thrown into a situation where I had no choice but to receive help, and I began to learn to ask for help. I was reminded of something I had heard in one of my Bible studies a few years back. When we don't let others help, we deny the giver the blessing of giving.

I slowly began asking my new community of friends to help. I had a small group that John Michael was comfortable with that would come and stay with him while I went to the apartment for a break. It was usually in the evening. For the first 30 days, the Shepherd Center provided an apartment right next door. But because we were there for much longer than that, we had to find somewhere to live. By the grace of God and the kindness and generosity of others, we had an apartment not more than five miles away. It was brand new and very convenient. The only problem was the Atlanta traffic. Some days it could take me up to 20 minutes just to get there. I would go to the apartment and go for a run, shower, eat dinner, and then return to Shepherd to stay the night. After about 6 weeks, I was strongly encouraged by family to hire someone to stay with John Michael during the night so I could get decent sleep. I found the sweetest lady, Carla, who became my lifeline. She came three nights a week to stay with him overnight and two late afternoons to stay with him until I returned around 10:00 p.m. She was a true blessing. She learned how to communicate with John Michael, and they enjoyed their movie nights. She called him her "baby boy."

I relied heavily on my friends Jack and Brandy, John Michael's friends Crosby and Gabby, and Ryan's friend Kirby to relieve me so I could get a break. Crosby is a fellow Under Armour teammate who was a face-off guy as well. He had John Michael cracking up on his visits or brought friends to entertain John Michael – just what the doctor ordered.

Crosby's father Edward stopped by often to say hello, offer help, and give John Michael encouragement. Edward always called John Michael FOGO. FOGO is a lacrosse term for face-off get-off. Typically, the face-off guy only faces off then gets off the field once possession has been established. I can still hear him say, "How's it going, FOGO?"

Gabby is the cousin of one of his longtime friends at home. John Michael is quite the ladies' man, so I know he enjoyed the female company. I always found it amazing that he had never met her until he arrived in Atlanta, and he never spoke a word to her that whole time, but they developed a close bond. One night when I returned from dinner, JM seemed extremely excited. I asked if he wanted to tell me something. He motioned yes. He proceeded to spell out, "Look under the sheet." I thought the nurse repositioned his legs like a pretzel and he was uncomfortable. When I pulled the sheet back there was a small gift bag. Inside was a beautiful cross necklace with a card that said, "Happy Valentine's Day, Mom. Love, John Michael." Gabby said he was too excited to wait until Valentine's Day. He then proceeded to spell out "I love seeing you happy." I guess the last time Gabby was there he told her to buy the necklace. Even during this horrific time, he still continued to amaze me! When he deserved to be selfish, he chose to think of others. That was the first time I cried in front of him.

CHAPTER 34

Friends

(John Michael)

My friends and girlfriend were unbelievably supportive. Whenever they *could* come to Atlanta, they *did*. I'm talking just about every weekend, not to mention the community of Atlanta who made us feel right at home. Crosby Matthews and Gabby Burns (both my age) are two people who would often come sit with me during the week when I was lying in bed, done for the day. They wanted to hang out, sure, but mostly to give my mom a break so she could leave, take a shower, and get some rest. Since probably eighth or ninth grade, Crosby and I lined up across from each other on the field in lacrosse tournaments. I'm going to level with you (he doesn't know this): I hated the guy. It was nothing to do with who he was as a person but solely because he was better than me! He became motivation. Fast forward a couple years and we were teammates on the Under Armour South lacrosse team. By now, I loved the guy. Crosby wore number 24 his senior year at Lovett High School.

Gabby, on the other hand, I did not know before my stroke. She is actually the cousin of my lifelong friend Piece Burns. So of course, her family living in Atlanta immediately reached out and when they came to visit, we hit it off. I guess even in this condition I have a terrible habit of attracting pretty blondes! (Don't get me wrong, Julia is a beautiful brunette – actually, most of my girlfriends were.) Needless to say, though, Gabby and I were able to connect despite the circumstances. She had the idea for me to get something for my mom for Valentine's Day. I'd like to say it was my idea, but it was Gabby's. I suggested a necklace and Gabby went and picked one out. When it came, she brought it to my room. When my mom came back, Gabby didn't say a word about it, leaving my mom to find the box next to me under the covers of my bed. That was a special moment I'll never forget.

Starting with my own high school, a few of the local high schools (including Julia's NSB high) all made videos in support. They were mostly comprised of individuals or groups of students/teachers saying hello, offering support, or throwing up a "24" with their hands. This became a common sign of support. Some of the people who did that included Arnold Palmer, Garth Brooks, and Lee Corso. Trinity was amazing.

I had everything from a car show to a 2.4K race organized to raise funds.

My room wasn't empty very long. The walls became covered in #24 jerseys (some signed) ranging from high school to pro. Not only did I receive numerous jerseys, but countless high school friends actually changed their sports number to 24, a trend that, for some, has continued into college.

I took a couple trips to Kennesaw State Stadium for some lacrosse games. You would think it might be too hard to watch, but I just couldn't get enough of it. I still love the game as if nothing happened. We rented a van and were technically on our own. It felt great to get out of there. We never went anywhere, though, without a tech who worked at the Shepherd Center, Rodney. Oh, Rodney! He was the best. He was one of the most genuinely funny guys I'd ever met. I honestly can't think of a time when he was upset or in a bad mood.

My first trip to the stadium was for a preseason tournament between four college teams including Notre Dame (admittedly my favorite D1 lacrosse team next to the Bears). My dad ended up with some fraternity brothers who had a connection to the team. I don't know how, but we got ND lacrosse shirts and hats with 24 on them. We were treated not only to box seats, but field passes for after the game. They couldn't have been nicer.

Mikey Wynne, #24 for the Irish, gave me a pair of his gloves that he signed. They are still in my room today.

On this day, it was wet, and we were rushed off the field because the Duke team was about to come out. During all the commotion Julia accidentally bumped the ND head coach with her umbrella! I was so embarrassed, but we had a good laugh about it later. We were also invited to go to the post-game team tailgate where I befriended PJ Finley, face-off guy for ND at the time.

My mom's college roommate's husband, Jack Jessen, lives in Atlanta and works in advertising. He often came to sit with me as well, and we became great friends. He was responsible for a lot of the outings I went on and jerseys I received in Atlanta. He got me a signed Devonta Freeman jersey (#24 for the Falcons and former Florida State Seminole). The first time I was without either of my parents (they were in Tallahassee for Ryan's graduation), he took me to a Georgia Swarm indoor lacrosse game. I was with Aunt Cedes (Mercedes), Aunt Ria (Big Maria), Uncle Bill, the Torrises (great friends from South Carolina), and of course, Rodney, so I was well taken care of. We were given a tour of the stadium, including the locker room and the field, and the team presented me with a lacrosse stick and a signed jersey. Along the way I had the absolute pleasure of meeting the Thompson brothers, which is a name anyone in lacrosse would know. During the game I had the spotlight shone on me in our box, and I was introduced over the loudspeaker.

We also went to a Hawks game where I got to go down on the court and see Kent Bazemore (#24), who had already visited the hospital. At the game I received a framed poster that he had signed. It remains in my room at home today. He came to Shepherd again to personally give me a signed jersey. On the day we left, the first floor elevators opened and there was Jack. He had already said goodbye but decided to come back to the hospital one more time and ironically, just at the right time.

I also went to a Braves game set up by Chip Caray, voice of the Braves and father of one of my elementary school friends (she was one of two very musically talented girls who actually made me a song while I was at Shepherd). Before the game, I got to go on the field and meet some of the players. My friend Jared got to come, and he absolutely loved it.

I had quite a few visitors during my time in Atlanta, including Casey Powell, Jimbo Fisher, Warrick Dunn, the Rollins women's lacrosse team, the UCF men's lacrosse team, and the Georgia Tech cheerleaders. I got a card from Tim Tebow, and we joked that we thanked God he didn't send a jersey! I even got a basketball signed by Shaq! All this stuff was great, but you know I'd trade it in a second for my life back.

CHAPTER 35

The Story of '24'

(John Michael)

Up until high school, I was #16 for obvious reasons. It was my graduation year as well as my birthday. My freshman season at Trinity, when it came time to choose jerseys, we went in order of seniority. I had grown up watching this kid from Maryland, Stephen Kelly, who wore 24. He ended up going to the University of North Carolina, and while only a few years older, I admired his aggressive style of play as a face-off man. When it came to my turn, there weren't many choices left and #16 was taken. Kelly was no doubt in the back of my mind when I chose 24, but I also truly believe it was meant to be.

Granted, Trinity Prep lacrosse is not the best. Far from it. We didn't even have a JV team. Nonetheless, I went on to start at the face-off position as a freshman on varsity. I wouldn't say I was a standout player, but I did pretty well, all things considered. The next year I would be named team captain as a sophomore. No one was touching the #24 jersey, and I never dreamt of changing it. The thought had never occurred to me because I wanted every opposing team and coach to know exactly what to expect every time they saw my number on the field.

One of the hardest moments for me was (and will always be) the realization that I wasn't going to play my senior season. Don't get me wrong, every day I have to deal with the fact that I may never fulfill my dream of playing Division I lacrosse, but that was a chapter of my life that hadn't even begun yet. I knew what it was like to have everyone's eyes on me. I knew what it was like to command the respect and attention of my teammates. I knew what that fellowship was like. That's something that I haven't been able to experience at Mercer. That's something that I never got to finish at Trinity… and when I start something, I intend to finish it.

I verbally committed to play at Mercer in the fall of my junior year, which some would say is early. But after visiting the school and meeting the coaches, I just knew. Plus, there was no way this Florida boy was going to school too far north! Mercer University is located in Macon, Georgia, so it's only about two hours away from the Shepherd Center in Atlanta. The head coach, Kyle Hannan, went above and beyond when he heard what happened. As well as visiting me at the Shepherd Center several times, he took the whole team down to *my* high school in Winter Park, Florida to put on a clinic and a preseason scrimmage on *my* field against Rollins College. I hadn't played a second for this man, and here he was, fundraising for me. Doing all this for me when his own son Kade has Tetralogy of Fallot with Pulmonary Atresia; Kade has had five heart surgeries. His daughter Margo even wore number 24 her senior year of girls' lacrosse at Stratford Academy.

Despite being just about the coldest weekend in Florida history, the turnout was unbelievable. It was live streamed for me to watch from my bed in Atlanta. That was hard to watch. Not only that, but the entire team (yes, the entire team) came to Shepherd on their way up to play Duke in Durham – all because I signed a piece of paper. They, of course, brought me a #24 Mercer Bears jersey they had all signed. Remember, I was in my senior year of high school, so these are a lot of the guys I looked up to, guys who were supposed to be my mentors. I really enjoyed that day, and if nothing else, it reaffirmed my decision in choosing Mercer to further my lacrosse career.

CHAPTER 36

Brad Pitt and Jesus

(JM Vickie)

The staff at the Shepherd Center is some of the best. They became our family, and we loved and appreciated all they did for us while we were there. Some of the stories we (and I'm sure they) could tell are pretty funny, while some are pretty aggravating.

Edith was the sweetest little lady. She was his CNA. She would come in every morning and proclaim, "Let's go, John Michaels! We got to go! You can't be late for Miss Ali!" She always called him John Michaels. When we first met her, I thought she was far too bossy and made me do most of the work. But by the time we left, I wanted to bring her home with us. She taught me so much and I will forever be grateful. She was making me do most of the work in preparation for what was to come once we were home.

The list of all his CNAs and nurses is long. There may have been a couple that we requested he not have (one smelled like a cigarette), but for the most part, they were amazing. Early on in our stay, when I had just come back to his room from dinner, the nurse came in and she said, "Hey Brad!" The "Brad" was very drawn out like "Braaaaad."

I said, "His name isn't Brad". She said, "Oh, I know honey, he's my Brad Pitt!" John Michael and I just died laughing. Most women who came into John Michael's room gave him a compliment on his good looks and just had to run their fingers through his hair; otherwise known as his flo. Many lacrosse boys wore their hair long and would refer to their hair as their flo. The boys like how it hung out of the back of their helmet. John Michael decided that he was not going to cut his hair until he left the Shepherd Center. It was pretty long to start with, but by the time we left, it was so long that we joked he looked like Jesus.

CHAPTER 37

Good and Evil

(John Michael)

Of all the cool things I received, an e-mail from the Pope has to be my favorite. A boy in my class has family who had connections, or something like that. Here is the e-mail we received:

From: San Pietro >   Hide

To: Amos Epelman >

P. Francis   ●
Today at 3:08 AM

Dear Vickie and Mick,
May the Peace of Christ be with you!
I heard about the health situation of your beloved son
John, and I want to express to you and John my
paternal closeness and assure you of my prayers.
When human hope ends, divine hope begins; when
all seems difficult, God always opens for us a
window of light and hope.

Please know that I am praying for John and for you.
I ask God to give all of you the courage of faith to
face this difficult moment with the power of the Holy
Spirit, and I entrust you to the maternal care of our
Blessed Mother.
May the Lord bless you, and please do not forget to
pray for me!

Francis

Ironically, in the same week, AC/DC made a video and
signed a shirt. My best friend Rowly's family has connections
with lead singer, Brian Johnson. The joke was that I have both
good and evil on my side, so I can't lose!

CHAPTER 38

With a Little Help from Our Friends

(JM Vickie)

Many of my close friends came as well to be with us and to give me a break. Several stayed in the room with him at night so I could get a good night's sleep. Just their presence was such a blessing to me. My friend Paige learned how to brush his teeth. Her husband David even took a turn with the toothbrush. My dear friend Cathy gave me the coat off of her back. My sweet friend Courtney came and stayed with me often just to be a blessing in any way she could.

The many visitors who came to visit is quite an extensive list. Frequent visitors, of course, were family, my close friends, his squad, friends from his high school/lacrosse team, Julia and many others. The first time his squad came to visit, they picked up right where they left off. Needing a break, we left John Michael with the squad while we went to grab some lunch.

On returning, we found them all in great spirits. Come to find out, while we were gone, the nurse had transferred him into his wheelchair. Just right outside of his door was a small kitchen with a refrigerator to keep food. There were name tags on the counter for patients and family to label their food. So while we were gone the boys took a label, wrote "Asshole" on it and put in on John Michael! They proceeded to wheel him around the floor while loudly playing the song "Riding Dirty." They, of course, thought this was hilarious. I thought we were going to get kicked out!

We pretty much took over the floor, especially when the University of Central Florida lacrosse team, the Lake Highland High School lacrosse team, the Georgia Tech cheerleaders, and members of the Face-Off Academy came to visit (all on different days, of course). Our family was thrilled when Warrick Dunn and Coach Jimbo Fisher came to visit. I am so very proud and impressed with how my university was so supportive during this time. But by far the most special visits came from the Mercer University lacrosse coaches, followed by a visit from the whole team!

I had taken John Michael to Macon, Georgia for his unofficial visit to Mercer University in the fall of his junior year. We had been on several other visits and were making the rounds. It was a great visit and John Michael left feeling pretty excited. Once we were back home for a few days, the coach called and offered him a position on the team. He thanked him and said he needed to talk to his parents. This was not his first offer, but we had several other schools on his list yet to visit. He came downstairs and declared to us that he wanted to commit to Mercer. We were a little surprised, given he was just a junior and not yet done with the recruiting process. We explained this to him, but also told him that this has been his decision and his goal all along, and if this is what he wanted to do, we were behind him 100%. That night, he picked up the phone and called Coach Hannan and committed to play lacrosse at Mercer University. At the time, I had no idea that this would be one of the best decisions of his life.

From the moment Coach Hannan heard of John Michael's devastating stroke, he was all in. He immediately began organizing a lacrosse event in John Michael's honor in our hometown. The whole team traveled down and played an exhibition game against Rollins College and then held a lacrosse clinic. Even though it was one of the coldest days in Winter Park history, the turnout was unbelievable. The event was held at John Michael's high school and was live streamed so we could watch from Atlanta. It was amazing. From the bake sale to the purple balloons and ribbons, shirts, wristbands, and all of the personal messages, it blew us away.

Later that month, Coach Hannan, along with the other coaches, came to visit us at Shepherd. It meant so much to

John Michael. He was very excited they brought along some Mercer gear! About a month later, the whole team came to visit. It was a sight to behold. The buses pulled up and out came about 50 young men who had never even stepped onto a field with John Michael. Some of them had helped to recruit him, but most had never even met him.

The Center let us use their large gathering room. The boys walked in carrying a #24 jersey for him. It was a special time for everyone. The local TV station was there to interview Coach Hannan, then Mick and me. It was the first time I had spoken publicly about John Michael. I was amazed I was able to hold it together. Mick, on the other hand, had a more difficult time. It was just too painful.

To this day, Coach Hannan and the boys come to Winter Park to play lacrosse in his honor. Everything they did made me come to realize why John Michael chose to commit to Mercer so quickly. These coaches and players are so dedicated to seeing John Michael through and giving him all the love and support he needs. They make him feel very much a part of the team, even though they have never played a second together.

JMStrong24

(Vickie)

We have always been a very active family – bike rides, jogging, hiking, surfing, paddle boarding, the list goes on. So to be stuck inside a facility all day, week after week, was excruciating, to say the least. Finally, we were cleared to take John Michael on our own outings as long as we took a staff member with us. Woo hoo! We were out of there!

We set up a transportation company for the wheelchair and found a staff member, Rodney, who John Michael loved, to tag along. Rodney was the man! Our first outing was, of course, a lacrosse game. There was a preseason exhibition game with four of the best teams in the country. One was Notre Dame. We, fortunately, had some connections, so we were treated to a box and were able to go onto the field after the game to meet the coach and the team. The player who wore #24 for Notre Dame gave him his gloves. They are on display on a shelf in John

Michael's room today. The best part is that a few of these Notre Dame players have stayed in touch with him. The face-off guy even wore JM on his helmet for him. Everyone was touched by his story.

Our next outing was to the Atlanta Hawks game. Thanks to our great friends Jack and Brandy, #24 Kent Bazemore came to visit him at the center. Jack arranged for us to go early and be on the court as they warmed up. Bazemore had written JMSTRONG24 on his shoes. He gave John Michael an autographed poster with his motto:

- Be Resilient

- Aspire to be Great

- Motivate Yourself

- Enjoy your Success!

John Michael would get to see Bazemore again once we were home in Orlando when the Hawks were in town to play the Magic. We spent some time with him before the game. He is a great man with a big heart. They even wrote an article about it in the Atlanta paper. His story continues to touch so many.

We were so grateful every time we were able to leave Shepherd and go somewhere. The walls really start to feel like they are closing in on you. Other outings included a couple of trips to a local high school to see his friend Crosby play lacrosse. One of those times they happened to be playing a high school from Orlando, so John Michael got to see many friends from home as well. More lacrosse outings included a trip to the Atlanta Blaze game and to the ACC Lacrosse Championship game. Our final trip was to see the Atlanta Braves. Our good friend Chip Caray set us up with jerseys, a meet and greet before the game with the players, and great seats. We really got spoiled on all those outings. It was like John Michael was a celebrity.

CHAPTER 40

The Many Blessings of Our Community

(Vickie)

Meanwhile, back at home, John Michael's high school, as well as the whole community, continued to support him holding many fundraisers. The school held a charity basketball game against their rival school. It was standing room only in the gym. They live streamed the game so we could watch. We cried as the headmaster spoke about John Michael and when the rival school presented him with a most generous check for John Michael's recovery. One school family put on a car show at the school to raise money. Each year the senior class picks a project, usually community-based. This year, they picked their classmate, John Michael. They organized a 2.4K run. The turnout was unbelievable. They raised $100,000! We were speechless.

Many other schools throughout the community held fundraisers as well. Ben's school, which is also our church community, sold T-shirts and wristbands, had bake sales and more to help. This made Ben feel important and helpful. Ben and John Michael are seven years apart. Ben has always looked up to John Michael, and they have a very special bond. He had just turned 11, and not thinking there was anything he could do, the high school and his friends helped him feel useful and special. Some of his friends even had lemonade stands in their neighborhoods. The support was endless, and I am sure I am forgetting, or may not even know, everything that was done to help. I just know I am forever grateful and wish I could personally thank each and every one who supported us. Hearing about (and knowing) all that was going on at home truly helped comfort us.

CHAPTER 41

Progress

(Vickie)

Atlanta is considered the South, but for people from Florida, the weather can be pretty cold. Once the weather began to turn, we made our way out into the garden area. At Shepherd, there was a pretty area they called the garden. As soon as John Michael was finished with therapy, we headed outside until we had to go back in for him to get his meds and get hooked back up to the feeding tube. The first warm day was the best. We both just sat there basking in the sun. He reclined in his chair and me on a bench. We just soaked in the warmth of the sun. I'm sure we were vitamin D deficient! At home we were always outside.

The garden was right next to the main road. I often thought about escaping, like I was in prison or something. I dreamed of wheeling John Michael right out of the gate and going somewhere, anywhere. You can't help but feel trapped when you are somewhere you don't want to be, even if you are there for a good cause. So we found our escape when we could in the garden and dreamed of being home on the warm beach with sand in our toes and not a worry in the world. We looked forward to our garden trips every day. We always tried to meet our new friends Allison and Rivers there. Allison was Ryan's age and she was always there with Rivers, her boyfriend since high school.

Rivers was another patient at Shepherd. Rivers could not speak or move much either, but you could tell by their eyes that John Michael and Rivers made a connection. We either met them in the garden, they would come to our room to visit, or we would venture down the hall to see them. It was often the highlight of our day, and it's how we ended our day. We'd head down around 4:00 p.m., and we typically only had an hour before we had to get back or they would come looking for us.

Although we often ended a day in the garden, each day began with therapy. Speech therapy usually consisted of exercises to help him swallow and vocalization exercises. We started with ice chips, then gradually moved to lollipops. A few weeks before we were due to return home, someone from home reached out to me about vital stim for the face. It helps strengthen the muscles to be able to swallow. I asked about it and was told it probably wouldn't help because it wouldn't recruit the muscles they were targeting. I said I wanted to do it anyway. Within one week, he passed his swallow study and was cleared for soft foods like pudding, mashed potatoes, and apple sauce. We were thrilled. In this world we are in, we have to try anything and everything. Once again, I was learning to stand up to the "experts" and demand things for John Michael.

In occupational therapy, they worked on isolated arm movements, keeping his head up while lying on his stomach, as well as sitting on the edge of a mat. He got pretty good at sitting on the edge of the mat but learned that he was using all tone to sit. We needed core strength to volitionally sit upright. I think physical therapy was his favorite. They did leg presses, standing in a standing frame, and walking, either on the treadmill or on the ground with a harness. The leg press was the easiest for him. The walking was beginning to look good, but he did not have the core strength or endurance to keep his head up.

Progress is what we were there for, and progress he did make, just not as much as we would have liked. In hindsight, and speaking honestly, when you are in a facility, they tend to have a routine, a regimen for everyone. I do believe this is necessary, but I also believe that not everyone is the same. If I had not been such a deer in the headlights, or still dealing with the shock, I may have realized at the time that John Michael was way too medicated. He knew this himself. Every time the doctor came to see him, he would always spell out, "No more meds." Once we were home and weaned him from several of the medications, we saw more progress. Again, this is in no way a discredit to the Center, just something we experienced in our case.

I would recommend the Shepherd Center to anyone, but I would also recommend going in more educated than I was. I also learned that the quality of care is related to the person sitting in the chair next to the patient. This goes for any hospital or rehab center. If it's your child, you have to be that momma bear, even if it makes you unpopular with the staff. There are days when they are understaffed and overworked, but on some days, the squeaky wheel gets the grease, and you don't get what you need until you ask.

CHAPTER 42

Attitude is Everything

(Vickie)

They say attitude is everything, and I am a strong believer in it. John Michael's senior quote from high school (before this happened) was, "Attitude reflects leadership." I am so very grateful that John Michael has had the most amazing attitude throughout his struggle. Once he started laughing in the PICU, he never stopped. When we arrived at Shepherd, we learned that his laughter was not always "appropriate," which it often times wasn't. The stroke affected his ability to control his emotions. Some stroke victims will cry, others will laugh, some may do both uncontrollably. I am so glad John Michael laughed! They did end up putting him on medication to help, but he was eventually weaned off. We did, however, laugh appropriately – a lot. I was told we were using laughter as a defense mechanism. I'm sure we were, but I'd rather laugh than cry any day of the week. Before we left the PICU, John Michael spelled out to me "Laughter takes the pain away." He was not, and never was, in any physical pain. He knew he'd rather laugh than cry as well.

John Michael had limited therapy on the weekends. On one of our first Saturdays there, the schedule said he would have OT. Normally all of his therapy, besides speech, was in the gym down the hall. My sister was visiting, and we were bored, so we decided not to wait on the therapist to come get him, but to head on down to the gym. Several other patients were arriving as well.

The therapist asked, "Are you here for OT?"

We replied, "Yes."

Next thing we know, we were in a circle with the other patients being told to do exercises. Now mind you, John Michael couldn't move, much less raise his arm, so we did the motion for him. I thought, "What on earth?" We had specifically told them that John Michael did not want group therapy. Someone was going to hear about this!

The more they asked the patients to move, the more John Michael laughed. He thought it was hysterical. My sister and I were trying so hard to keep it together, but in the end, the three of us were bursting out laughing, looking like a bunch of idiots.

Just then, I heard, "Are you John Michael? I am the OT. I've been looking for you." She had come to his room to get him for therapy, but we had already left. John Michael was about to kill us! Looks like I wouldn't be complaining after all. My sister and I laugh about it to this day.

Ryan hated that she could not be there with John Michael as much as she wanted. Soon after his stroke, it was time for her to return to Florida State and finish her last semester. She didn't want to go. Mick and I strongly encouraged her to finish strong. This is what John Michael wanted, too. She felt helpless in Tallahassee, so she organized a fundraiser through her sorority. It was called "Oh, What a Night." It was a dessert fundraiser for her brother's recovery. The girls in the sorority baked all the desserts and many came. The line was way out the front door of her sorority house! Not only did so many students attend, but the president of the University, John Thrasher, and Coach Jimbo Fisher stopped by.

Mick and I both graduated from FSU many moons ago. It's where we met and fell in love. We later were married and had three amazing children. Our children may be spread apart in age, but the bond they have with each other is extremely close. We were so proud of Ryan for how hard she worked to pull off this event. She is an awesome sister, and John Michael loves her dearly.

About a month before we came home, we went to Tallahassee to celebrate Ryan's college graduation from Florida State University! We were so proud of her for finishing strong. She graduated cum laude! John Michael was able to watch a video we sent him. He was on his way to the Georgia Swarm indoor lacrosse game as she was crossing the stage. On her way across the stage, Ryan held up a big 24 with her fingers to the camera. It was perfect! We all held it together pretty well until we tried to take a family photo and it just wasn't right. There was a big gaping hole! The tears flowed. But God is good, and he helped us pull it together and focus on our other wonderful child and what a joy and a blessing she is to our family.

CHAPTER 43

Rising Up

(Vickie)

Easter came while we were at Shepherd. They had a beautiful service in the large gathering room where we had met the Mercer team. This Easter service was, of course, about the Resurrection, but not just the resurrection of Jesus. It was about each patient and their resurrection from the tragedy they had faced. We all go through hard times, obviously some worse than others, and we can choose to stay in our tomb or chose to be resurrected. Your resurrection may not look exactly as you expect or hope, but you will be okay. You can rise above your tragedy. God created you to rise above it, but not alone.

There was actually a service every Sunday at 1:00. John Michael and I always went. There were service dogs at the Center, and we always requested Frosty on Sunday mornings. Frosty looked a lot like our dog at home, Baylor. We took him to the service with us, but on Easter Sunday our whole family, as well as Little Maria's family, was there. It was a special time. They stayed for several days. It was by no means the Easter we were used to, but this year, just like Christmas, it was more of what it is supposed to be – more about Jesus. I didn't have a home to decorate or eggs to color, I didn't even buy baskets. Normally we would have been at our beach condo, attending mass, going to brunch, then having the annual Easter egg hunt. I felt bad for Ben and Grace. They were only 10 and still wanted to have the hunt. My sister bought eggs, but no one was really in the mood.

The following week, they were still there, and one day, during John Michael's therapy, he was out of his bed and in the gym down the hall. I walked back into his room to get something, and I found Ben in John Michael's bed and Grace was standing beside him with the dry erase board. They were playing "John Michael." Grace asked Ben a question, and Ben answered by blinking his eyes to the letter board to spell out the word, just like his brother. It was such a precious moment that I am so glad I walked in on.

CHAPTER 44

Coming of Age

(Vickie)

John Michael turned 18 that March. All of his friends came, as well as family and local friends we had made in Atlanta. We again used the large meeting room. We brought in pizza and cake for all. It was a fun time and John Michael was so excited to open his gift from Coach Jimbo Fisher. He sent John Michael a signed #24 FSU jersey with Night on the back. We hung it in his room as soon as we got back.

All seemed to be going well until it was time for cake. John Michael finally broke down. I say "finally" because he had yet to really cry. Never in a million years would I have dreamed I'd be spending John Michael's 18th birthday helping give him a shower, encouraging him to move or watching him try and operate a wheelchair with his chin using a joystick. Really? How could this be? I'll never fully understand. It will never make sense.

Eighteen years ago, that day my sweet boy came into this world and brought me so much joy, love and laughter, and he hasn't stopped. We are very similar in personality and share a special bond. He's my easygoing child whose life just got very complicated. I don't know how he does it. From never complaining to trying harder every day, he is just amazing. This definitely wasn't where or how he wanted to spend his 18th birthday, but there we were, and we made the best of an otherwise sad time. We decided to make it a celebration of his progress and his unwavering determination to get his life back.

Back at home, a fundraising event was held for John Michael on Park Avenue, our "main street" with lots of shops and restaurants. Many of the vendors donated a percentage of their sales that day to John Michael. The Avenue was decorated with purple ribbons on all of the trees, purple balloons, and many stores displayed JM shirts in their windows. Many took pictures holding the number 24 and posting it on his Facebook page.

CHAPTER 45

The Prom

(Vickie)

Missing the second half of his senior year was very hard for John Michael, as it would be for anyone. It's the best part of senior year. So many events and ceremonies took place (not to mention lacrosse season) while he was gone, one of which was prom. At the time of his stroke, John Michael was dating Julia. Julia is a beautiful girl, full of life and faith. I often say that I do not think people realize what she went through when her boyfriend stroked. It was like something out of a movie. She was only 17 and so in love with my son, the all-American athlete loved by everyone, who had just suffered a massive tragedy. They were inseparable. They were the perfect couple. She is one of six children and fit right in with our family.

We did not tell her John Michael had stroked until we found out exactly what had happened. It was very early

Thursday morning that I called her stepmom at the time to tell her so she could prepare Julia for the devastating news. Her father immediately drove her to the hospital. They had to pull over because she was physically ill.

Julia's family lives in New Smyrna, about an hour away. She and John Michael had met through mutual friends. We have a beach condo in New Smyrna, so they would see each other often. After she had been at the hospital nonstop for a few days, her dad and I felt she needed to go home and rest. Needless to say, just like the rest of us, she was a mess. She wasn't eating or sleeping. We finally had to make her leave the hospital. She was not happy, but it truly was for her best interests.

While we were in the PICU, she was there as often as she could be. When we were at Shepherd, she came several times to visit. My favorite memory was of the prom. She chose not to go to her own senior prom even though John Michael assured her that it was okay with him if she went. I even tried to encourage her to go, but she was not interested in going without John Michael. The weekend of John Michael's prom, she came to visit. It was the sweetest thing ever. They had their own special prom night. She brought a beautiful dress and brought John Michael a shirt that looked like a tux. She even brought a boutonniere and corsage. It wasn't anything close to what prom should've been, but it is a prom they will never forget.

Julia was a tremendous help to me and John Michael. She was someone he could talk to that wasn't his mother or even his guy friends. She asked the tough questions that even I was afraid to ask. I will forever be grateful to her.

When it was time for her to head off to college, John Michael decided he needed to let her go. He spelled out to me a letter for her. I felt like I was breaking up with her! When she came over, he had me put the letter on his lap and had her come into his room. I'm sure it took her by surprise, but I have to say, the letter was very thoughtful and mature for someone so young. Basically, he told her that she needed to go to college and have fun, not be worried about him all the time or feel like she had to come home every weekend. He said that he needed to concentrate on getting better, and she needed to have a full college life.

She took it pretty hard as you can imagine, but I'm sure if you asked her today, she would admit it was the right thing to do. John Michael and Julia are still friends and she often visits when she is in town. She will always hold a special place in our hearts.

CHAPTER 46

Some Things are Just Not Fair

(Vickie)

While we were at Shepherd, they had senior night for John Michael's high school lacrosse team. It was such a great group of guys that we had enjoyed watching over the years. It broke my heart that John Michael had to miss it. I was just as sad as he was about not being there. Watching my son play a sport he loved and was so dedicated to had been one of the greatest joys of my life. I had cheered him on as he ran down that field so many times, and now I found myself cheering when he moved anything. I had looked forward with pride to walking him out on that field. I now looked forward to him walking anywhere! Life is so crazy and so unfair at times.

A few weeks before we were set to leave, we had John Michael's final chair fitting. He would be going home in a powered wheelchair. We tried many different devices for him to be able to operate his chair independently and found that the head array was the easiest. To no one's surprise, he mastered it very quickly. They initially set it to the slowest speed, but John Michael immediately figured out how to increase the speed and, being the teenager that he was, he sped down the hallways in the same way he drove his truck! You always knew when he was coming because he would put the chair in fast mode, take off down the hall and crack up laughing the whole way!

While he was getting fitted for his chair, he became very frustrated. You see, he was going home, and his high school graduation was just around the corner. He didn't want to cross the stage in a chair. He had claimed that he would walk to get his diploma, and now that goal seemed to be fading away. While he could laugh, have fun and make the best out of this awful circumstance, he couldn't ignore the reality of everything he had to miss out on.

CHAPTER 47

Places to Go

(John Michael)

I went on several outings during my time at Shepherd. The first one was about a week after we got there. They were going to the college football hall of fame, and my recreational therapist, Liz, asked if I wanted to go. I said yes. My mom asked me probably 50 times leading up to it if I was sure I wanted to go and then another 50 on the day of the outing. My mom, Liz and I had gone to a CVS across the street in preparation for it. That was my first time in public since the stroke. So I went, and it's a decision I'd make again.

One by one they loaded us up into the large van. I actually wore a neck brace because it was my first time sitting up in a car. When we got there, I told Liz I wanted to keep it on. I'm not quite sure I needed it, but I think it was more of a comfort thing. I can only imagine what people thought when they saw such an eclectic (injury-wise) group of mostly young men in wheelchairs, but I didn't care what people thought of me. I didn't think twice when I got a second look. I knew who I was. I knew what I had accomplished, what I was going to accomplish, and what I will now accomplish. The only judgment I cared about comes from the One who put us here and chooses to wake us up every day.

> *Do not judge, or you too will be judged.*
> -MATTHEW 7:1

The only negative of the trip was that on the way back we stopped at Chick-fil-a so everyone could eat – everyone except me. I just sat there and watched as they ate my favorite meal. I have no clue what the thought process was there. Those close to me couldn't even bring themselves to eat in the room with me, much less Chick-fil-a.

One positive thing from being at Chick-fil-a was that I sat next to a guy named Austin who had a spinal cord injury. We weren't the only two at the table, of course, but somehow, we became friends without me saying a word. Since my injury was considered a brain injury, I was on the third floor with the ABI patients. The therapy gym was so dark and quiet with the blinds closed and no music. It was not an ideal atmosphere for a completely cognitive 17-year-old boy trying to work hard.

I remember my first time in there I got scared and upset. Where am I? Who are these people? My occupational therapist,

Karla, was trying to comfort me. She decided to go ahead and start. She put the electrodes on the top of my forearm and turned on the stim. My wrist went up. That was honestly the first time I had seen one of my body parts move or go through the full range of motion like that without someone touching it. I started to settle down. *Breathe, you can do this,* I thought.

Anyway, I would often visit Austin up on the fourth floor (SCI) during recreational therapy. It was a whole different world up there. All the blinds were open and there was upbeat music playing. With Liz's help, we played all kinds of board games with some of the other patients. I really enjoyed my time up there.

One time in recreational therapy we went out to the garden for some games. My mom and I loved the garden; it was our little haven. When we first got there, we wouldn't have dreamed of spending time outside in the cold, but as time went on and I was out of bed more frequently, we relished our time sunbathing in the garden. It was embarrassing how vitamin D deficient these Floridians were.

Anyway, there were several stations set up out there. Liz and I chose bocce ball. She picked up the ball, placed it in my hand, and then helped me swing my arm forward. I looked around. What was this? What am I doing here? I'm surrounded by people in wheelchairs, most of whom need help to do anything and half of whom didn't know the difference between bocce ball and basketball. Don't get me wrong, a brain injury is a very sad thing, but in my head, I was still a Division I athlete. I didn't belong here. This wasn't right.

Toward the end of my stay, my best friends, Rowly and Jared, came up to learn how to help me walk in preparation for graduation. I cannot tell you how grateful I am to Trinity that they allowed me to graduate despite not having attended school for the better half of my senior year. It certainly helped that it was a small school. I had been going there since sixth grade, I had an older sister who paved the way for me and was well connected, and my best friend's dad was the principal, not to mention that this type of thing literally doesn't and should never happen to anyone.

It took three people to walk me – one on each leg and one behind holding and controlling my hips. Originally it was going to be the two guys and my dad, but I knew my dad was going to be emotional (as we all were), so I wanted it to be only my classmates. I made the decision to go to my other best friend, Jake. Jake and I were close before, but he was about to become, hands down, one of my closest friends.

When it came time to leave, we ordered our own chair and I went to their seating clinic to have everything adjusted. Turns out a wheelchair is not just a wheelchair. You'd be amazed by the things that go into it and all the different parts and pieces that are custom for my body. I started to get upset during this. I was going home in a wheelchair. Once again, it all became real.

Like the PICU, it felt like we were there for so long. The normal amount of time for someone to be at Shepherd was about six weeks. We were there for a little over five months. The deal was that we could stay as long as I was progressing, and seemingly every time they tried to get us to leave, something new came about. We headed home, fittingly, on May 24th. I started at CORE the 25th.

Chapter 48

Going Home

(JM Vickie)

Once again, the day came to leave. This was much harder than leaving the PICU. We were not only saying goodbye to everyone at Shepherd, but to all of our friends and support in Atlanta. So many bonds were formed or strengthened while we were there. When we left Winter Park, I knew we'd be returning and would see everyone soon. Leaving Atlanta, we didn't know when we would see anyone again. We relied so much on everyone there and will never forget all that was done for us.

We purchased an accessible van for when we got home. Mick's brother drove this home for us. Mick's dad drove my car. We had arrived with one bag apiece and left with two cars loaded down! It was full of the many things that were given and sent to us. On our last night, there I was lying on the makeshift bed in his room and once again, I was scared to death. It was a different kind of scared. We were going home! I would have help 24/7. No longer would we have to wait for the nurse or wait for therapy. It was all planned out. But we weren't supposed to be going home like this, still in a chair, still unable to talk or eat. This time, though, I thought, "I can do this. So it takes a couple of years at best; I've got this."

That last morning, instead of being awoken by the nurse to take his vitals, we were greeted by Stan and a few of his favorite nurses. They called themselves "Stan and the Brainettes." They had made up a song called "John Michael Strong." The lyrics went something like this: "John Michael Strong / You're moving on, John Michael Strong / John Michael Night, you're up for the fight / You're flying high like a big old kite, John Michael Night." We all just laughed. It was very fitting that we started with Stan and we ended with Stan, our guardian angel.

Ryan and I were the only ones there that last day with John Michael. It felt like we had been there for a lifetime. We loaded the last bit in my car and sent Grandpa on his way. Mick made sure John Michael had some therapy that day, since the plane was not due to take off until around 3:00 p.m. We bought pizza for everyone on the floor and celebrated our time there.

Our transportation for the airport arrived early. This is where everything started spinning out of control. We were not ready. I just remember rushing back to his room to collect the last few items. Any supplies for John Michael in the room were ours to take. I did not realize this. As we were leaving, giving last minute hugs and waving goodbye, Edith handed us items to take with us. We were not even paying attention. All of a sudden, I looked over at Ryan and started laughing. She was waving goodbye with a handful of condom catheters! It still makes us laugh whenever we talk about that day.

With tears in our eyes, we loaded onto the elevator. As the doors opened, there was Jack. I mentioned Jack earlier as a friend who helped us out. Jack and John Michael became friends – good friends. Jack not only organized many of our outings, but he stayed with John Michael often to give me a break. He loved John Michael as his own and was going to miss his time with him. He had already said his goodbyes but had to come back for one last hug. He was another person to whom John Michael had never spoken but had a deep bond with. Fortunately, Jack is married to Brandy, my college roommate, so we have seen them a few times since we left.

Once again, we boarded a medical jet, but this time we were going home! It had been a long time since John Michael had been in his own house. He was ready. He couldn't wait to see everyone and be in familiar surroundings. Going outside whenever he wanted, going to bed whenever he wanted, and going to new therapy were a few of the things he looked forward to. The flight was fairly quick, and this time seamless, with no issues of needing oxygen. Mick, Ben, and Julia met us at the airport with the new van and his chair.

Our community had organized a Welcome Home parade for John Michael. There were even media vans at the airport to greet us. This was a bit overwhelming, especially for John Michael. When I heard they had organized a parade, I was just thinking of a few friends and classmates waving from the sidewalk off the main street through our downtown. But when we turned the corner onto Park Avenue, we were not ready for what saw!

CHAPTER 49

The Parade

(Vickie)

Just when I thought I was getting emotionally and physically stronger, the reality of being home hit me like a ton of bricks. It all started with the parade. It felt like the whole town turned out to welcome us home! The street was packed. Everyone was waving, cheering and chants of JMStrong could be heard all the way down our little main street.

Park Avenue is its name. There are many restaurants and quaint shops on this half-mile stretch. That day it felt like five miles. If I'm being honest, it was quite overwhelming. It's not that I didn't appreciate the support, but the reality of how public my life had become felt like too much to process. I just sat in the back of the van sobbing! So many people. I do not remember too many faces, but I will never forget John Michael's pre-school teacher, Mrs. Spangler, standing there waving with tears in her eyes.

The number of people who turned out for the parade was such a testimony to how far-reaching John Michael's story had become and how God was using this tragedy for His good. The street was lined with people and purple ribbons. Our church is on one of the last corners of the street, so it was the most crowded, mostly with John Michael and Ben's friends. Ben's school, K-8, had just let out. To see the little ones waving and cheering was so awesome. There were so many wearing their JMStrong shirts. We had seen pictures and heard stories of all of the love and support from home, but to see it first-hand was surreal.

As we turned the corner to head home, the ribbons did not end. They were everywhere! I think just about every tree was wrapped in a purple ribbon, and I have to tell you, the streets of Winter Park are all lined with oak trees. On several corners stood more friends, out to cheer us on and welcome us home. When we finally pulled into the drive, I think it truly hit us that we were home. John Michael was home! I could not stop the tears.

Looking back, I honestly don't know if they were tears of joy or tears of sadness that John Michael wasn't going to be walking back into the house. Sadness because we had to turn my beautiful dining room into his bedroom, and he would not be walking up the stairs to go to his own room. Sadness because he would have to shower in the newly built bathroom attached to the garage outside. Sadness because I traded my cute SUV and designer purse for a minivan and a backpack with supplies for John Michael. I'd like to think there were more tears of joy cried that day, but I cannot really say there were. This wasn't how it was supposed to be. We were supposed to come home with John Michael all better, not with an uncertainty of how much longer this was going to take.

We were first greeted at the house by a police officer who was there to make sure we did not have any unwanted guests. With all the attention we had received, we did not want anyone, friends included, just showing up. Also, there was a good deal of local media coverage. One cameraman actually came very close to the van and put the camera in the window that was rolled down on John Michael's side. This really upset John Michael. They also showed up later at the house as well. While we appreciated the coverage, because awareness was our goal, we needed our space to be together privately with just our family and John Michael's closest friends. We needed a couple of days to adjust to being home. Re-entry wasn't going to be easy.

When we unloaded everyone from the van, there he was – Baylor, our sweet, seven-year-old white lab! John Michael had missed him so much. It was evident that Baylor had missed him too. They used to lay on the couch together and Baylor loved when John Michael would take him for rides in his truck.

One night when I came home late from the PICU, I just sat with Baylor and cried. It felt like he cried, too. He knew and sensed that something was very wrong. The moment he saw John Michael, though, he was the happiest dog I had ever seen. He loved to get in bed with John Michael anytime he could. He would just lay as close to him as possible.

Unfortunately, after we had been home about a year, Baylor developed a tumor in his hip and ended up passing away just shy of his ninth birthday. It was a sad day in our house. John Michael was devastated. Man's best friend, a boy and his dog, these were all true of John Michael and Baylor. Our house has not been the same since he died. We still miss him every day.

We were also greeted by one of the caretakers who would be helping with John Michael. This was, and continues to be, one of my biggest struggles. John Michael does not need medical attention. He is extremely healthy, only taking a few medications during the day. John Michael is now a thriving, almost-22-year-old man. He is not looking for a caregiver to be his friend. He does not want someone there all the time, and neither do I. We like our space and our privacy. As sweet as they have been and as helpful as they are, I do not want someone all up in my business!

I am fortunate enough to have a housekeeper once a week. I do not even like being home when they are there. When the kids were little and I had a sitter, I'd leave as soon as she arrived. I do not like to be in my house when other people who are helping are there. I think a part of it is my type A personality. No one is going to do it like I would, so I'd rather not watch. Also, I do not like being a boss. I hate managing people. This has been a big learning curve for me as well. It is very hard to find the right personality fit for me, and especially John Michael.

We have been through our fair share of caretakers over the last three years. I've actually sent someone home at 1:30 in the morning! Everyone was asleep, and we heard John Michael screaming. There is a couch in his room for the caretaker to sit and rest. Her responsibilities are to get him ready for bed and listen for him throughout the night in case he needs to turn or be readjusted. So when we heard him screaming, we immediately ran downstairs. The room was dark, and the caretaker was just sitting on the couch.

When we asked her why she wasn't helping him, she said she didn't know what he wanted. We had taught her the communication system and also explained that she could ask yes or no questions. I also let her know that she could text me if she needed help and I would come down. When I asked John Michael, he said she hadn't even tried to figure out what was wrong. Needless to say, she left immediately. It has been incredibly hard to find the right fit. It's not a very difficult job;

actually, it's quite boring. I just need the help so I can have breaks and a life.

Most caretakers are used to working with the elderly. If I am home while the caretaker is there, John Michael would prefer me to help, depending on the need. But for the most part, he needs a drink of water, something to eat, needs help going to the restroom, or wants to get standing in his chair. The only time I most definitely want help is during the night. I like my sleep. I need my sleep. John Michael is not yet able to completely roll to both sides. If he gets uncomfortable in the middle of the night, he needs help repositioning himself. I value my nighttime caretakers. I would choose night help over daytime help any day of the week. That said, I do need a break during the day. I need time to exercise, have lunch with friends, spend time with Ben, or help at his school. I really need the help to just feel normal. I still haven't figured out exactly what that looks like, but I also still hang on to the hope that someday soon, we will no longer need the help!

CHAPTER 50

Not a Second Wasted

(Vickie)

When I say we did not waste any time jumping head-first into therapy, we did not waste a second. He started first thing the next morning with speech. Shannon, his speech therapist, came to the house to do an initial evaluation. She is truly amazing. John Michael and Shannon have developed a close friendship. Her hard work and dedication (and willingness to think outside the box) are the reason John Michael was able to get off the feeding tube. She is always ready with some new gadget or device. There is barely enough time during their sessions to do half of them.

Getting off of the feeding tube was a huge milestone. It was no easy feat. We spent hours eating. It would take 30 minutes to eat yogurt, and a real meal might take an hour. It felt like the majority of my day was spent feeding him. But it was well worth it to get off that tube! Once we knew he was getting sufficient calories, we focused on drinking water. We had to thicken it for a while. He hated it! I'm sure he used it as motivation. Within a few weeks he was cleared for water. The tube was coming out! We were excited beyond belief. We were initially told that he would be on a feeding tube for the rest of his life. I rebuked those words at the time and I then praised God that He heard me and answered.

John Michael picked this scripture to share on his Facebook page after the tube was removed. He said he felt "free," praising God for answered prayer.

"In my anguish I cried to the Lord, and he answered by setting me free. The Lord is with me, I will not be afraid." – Psalm 118:5-6

He wanted to mail the tube to those who said he would never get off of it and would only be able to eat pleasure food like pudding. But we are not vindictive people, so we let it go. Actually, it smelled so bad, I could have never sent it to anyone. The credit definitely went to his hard work and to Shannon and the Vital Stim! I was told it would not work. We did it five days a week once we got home and within four months, the tube came out. I have and will continue to recommend Vital Stim to anyone who has trouble swallowing. It was a game changer for John Michael.

Once we accomplished that, the focus became speaking. I am happy to say it is coming! We rarely, if ever, use the communication board to spell words. His voice may be quiet, and we may do a lot of lip reading, but he is talking. For the first couple of years, we actually had another speech therapist as well, Rachel. Shannon focused on eating and swallowing, and Rachel focused on vocalization and speaking. They were an awesome team. Unfortunately, life happens, and Rachel needed to focus on her full-time job and her three small children. We miss her dearly and are so appreciative of all she did for John Michael. She is a huge part of why John Michael is speaking. While we continue to perfect his speech, we are concentrating on drinking from a straw as well. It's funny how something that seems so simple could be so hard. It is amazing how many muscles it takes to speak, eat, and drink. I have learned so much. I am in awe of all his therapists and their training.

Once we finished with speech, we loaded up in the van and headed for his physical therapy. It was a place called CORE, Center for Recovery and Exercise. Once again, I had no idea what to expect. We were immediately greeted by Malerie, the Executive Director. Right away, she made us feel welcome and hopeful. She gave us a tour and explained their programs.

They began an evaluation of John Michael's capabilities. They had never worked with a locked-in patient before. Most people have not. They didn't know what to expect. Just like everyone else, they were amazed at our communication system. Thankfully, they also took the time to learn the letter board.

CORE has all of the equipment to get John Michael up and moving. Their first goal was to strengthen John Michael's core muscles and improve his head control. It was more like a gym that he was used to, not a facility. There was workout equipment and music that John Michael appreciated. He had two hours of therapy there, Monday through Friday. Several of the trainers actually do things socially with John Michael and have become his good friends. They come over and hang out or take him to a movie. It takes very special people to dedicate their lives to helping others regain theirs or adjust to a new way of life.

Many clients at CORE are spinal cord injuries. When you are not in "this world," you don't think about the fact that most people in wheelchairs can't just go to a normal gym and work out. So CORE is their gym to stay strong and fit. On days when I feel sorry for myself or John Michael, all I have to do is look around and see the many tragedies. I think every person in that gym was living a "normal" life until some tragedy took it from them. It is an incredible place full of hope and acceptance. It's not too far from our house, and I never knew about it. I never knew about a lot of things in this adaptive world, but what I have learned has humbled me and taught me to never take anything in life for granted, not even breathing.

When we arrived at the gym for John Michael's PT one morning, I was really having a low moment. I was full of self-pity and sorrow for John Michael, wondering where our lives had gone and how and why we got here. But as I sat in the gym and looked around, there were two very young boys, one seven years old and the other eight. Both were paralyzed – one from the waist down, and the other like John Michael, but he could speak. It was gut wrenching to hear one of them say he just wanted to play. The other was working hard for candy afterward. They were amazing. Just like John Michael, they worked so hard and had great attitudes. One boy said to the other, "Keep working hard. You'll get better." You have to love the faith of a child. Count your blessings indeed. I am so grateful John Michael had 17 years of play and lots of candy!

Our next stop was a rehab facility for his occupational therapy. John Michael loved Doro the OT, but he hated the facility. He was, by far, the youngest person. It was too quiet and very stark. Every time we would go, he would tell me he was not going back, not because he didn't like Doro, but because he hated the facility. We did stop going to the facility, but about a year later, he was so happy when she opened her Neurohub at CORE. Doro is an outside-the-box thinker, very creative, and extremely smart. I've often said that I think you have to be part engineer to be an OT. I send her studies and information on devices for her to research for me because when I read the studies, I don't understand half of the words! She is always contacting companies hoping to trial their devices or be part of a study. She has never made us feel hopeless or that John Michael would never regain the use of his hands or arms.

We eventually got connected with some awesome in-home neuro therapists as well. While CORE is amazing and has all of the necessary equipment, they are not neurologically trained and John Michael does have a brain injury, so we supplemented with therapists at home. Jen, another occupational therapist, and Stacey, a physical therapist, come to our home three times a week. Our garage was always set up as a mini gym for John Michael to work out. It has now been turned into a therapy room. We have a large work mat, a treadmill, and an overhead harness system, not to mention numerous pads, wedges, balls, stimulation systems, and more. Jen and Stacey co-treat John Michael for two hours, three times a week. They are some of the best at their jobs.

Eventually, we began to settle into a routine. It was a busy schedule, but John Michael preferred it to sitting there doing nothing, and he knew if he didn't use it, he would lose it! After we had been home a week, it was graduation time.

While at Shepherd, John Michael's friend Jared and his father, the principal at the time, came to visit. While they were there, John Michael spelled out, "Remember these words, I will walk at graduation." At the time, it meant he had three months to make it happen.

CHAPTER 51

Graduation

(Vickie)

Graduation came after we had only been home for a little over a week. The night before was rehearsal, and I was quickly learning that to get anywhere even remotely on time I would need a couple of hours to get myself and John Michael ready and loaded up in the van. So of course, we were late to the rehearsal.

When we walked into the auditorium, the senior class was seated in the first few rows and the principal was on stage. It was very quiet as the students listened to their instructions. As we started to make our way to the front, John Michael burst out laughing. I know I have said we laughed a lot and that laughing was a bit of an uncontrollable emotion for John Michael, but his laugh was so loud, and it sounded like a barking seal. Those who knew John Michael well were used to this sound, but for those who had never heard it, they did not know what to think!

His friends immediately started cracking up; John Michael was back.

We practiced exactly how it would go and what everyone needed to do to make it happen. John Michael had me give the principal a written statement that he wanted him to read at the end of the ceremony. We made it through rehearsal and went home to prepare for the big day.

For a day that should have been full of excitement and anticipation of the next chapter in John Michael's life, it was a bittersweet day. It is hard to find the words to describe what it actually felt like. As I helped John Michael shower, I was overwhelmed with sadness. Your mother is not supposed to be getting you ready on your graduation day. He should have been getting ready on his own and meeting his friends there early. I remember thinking how cruel and unfair it was as I helped get him dressed. I just kept asking, "Why God? Why?"

As we finally headed out to the graduation, John Michael wanted to add something to his statement. At Trinity, their motto is "Ad Astra Per Espera," which means "To the stars through difficulties" or "Through hardships to the stars." It was very fitting, especially given his situation. But then, he added "Momma, we made it!" As he spelled it out to me, tears flooded my face. I could not keep them from coming. You see, once again, here I was thinking how unfair this was, and he was thinking I made it! He just amazes me with his spirit and positive attitude.

We thought we had arrived early, but when we got there, the students were already lining up and about to take their class picture. The students would process in and be seated on the stage in the auditorium. John Michael would have to go around to the back to get onto the stage. Mick stayed with him in case he needed anything before Jared stood him up to receive his diploma. They also decided that John Michael would go last. It was going to be very emotional for everyone, and they did not want to take away from the students who would come after him. When the time came, Jared stood him up and his three best friends helped him take every step, sometimes even carrying him. It was too much. I just sobbed! Every single person in the auditorium cheered, clapped, and cried. There was not a dry eye in the building.

It was the most amazing event I have ever witnessed, a true miracle and blessing wrapped into one. There were so many answered prayers. The courage it took to take those steps is beyond comprehension. Mick and I have never been prouder. The look on his face was one of laughter and tears with sighs of joy and heartache. Indeed, he is my hero!

I have to give the biggest heartfelt thank you to Rowland Evans, Jared Herron, and Jake Moll. There are no words to adequately describe their dedication to their friend. Their demonstration of true friendship was incredible. It was a great reminder of the scripture I have claimed for John Michael, Luke 5:17-26, when several friends lowered their paralyzed friend on a mat through a roof so Jesus could heal him. It ends with Jesus telling him he is healed because of their faith: "Just then, some men came carrying a paralyzed man on a mat." Jesus saw their faith, forgave their sins, and healed their friend. My favorite part is when Jesus says, "I tell you, get up, take your mat, and go home." It ends with, "We have seen remarkable things today."

I truly felt like I had watched the gospel play out right before my eyes. This was also their big day, but they selflessly refused to do it without their friend. They were determined to find a way to get their friend across that stage just as the men in this scripture were determined to find a way to get their friend inside to see Jesus. It was remarkable indeed.

CHAPTER 52

Are You Listening, God?

(Vickie)

O ur first major outing was shortly after we were home. We headed over to New Smyrna Beach for Julia's graduation. We took one of the caretakers with us. Again, we barely made it. I was beginning to realize that I needed to allot more than two hours to the whole process or accept the fact that we were always going to be making it by the skin of our teeth. I have always hated being late. I was having to learn to give myself grace and realize it is okay. Even if being late disappoints someone or we miss part of something, it is okay.

We had a couple of situations occur during that outing that made me realize how much help I needed. We were no longer in the comfort of the Shepherd Center where I could just call for someone to help. I had to figure it out on my own. Even though I had help, they had never worked with a locked-in patient. They were looking to me for guidance and instruction, and honestly, I was making it up as I went, trying to act like I knew what I was doing when most times I didn't have a clue.

A typical day in the beginning went about like this: the day nurse arrived between 8:00 and 9:00 a.m., depending on JM therapy time. We administered JM medicine and got him up in his shower chair, then out to shower him. After his shower, we got him dressed and ready for the day, brushed his teeth, shaved, and so on. The whole process took an hour to an hour and a half and required two people.

I would then give him something to eat before we were off to therapy. His physical therapy at CORE was two hours long. To go anywhere, I had to give myself 30 minutes on both ends. After CORE, we headed home for more medicine and lunch. He then had speech therapy and occupational therapy. Sometimes the therapists came to the house, but other times we had to load back up and head out. By this time, it would be pushing 4:00 or 5:00 p.m.

After dinner, he liked to stand in his standing frame for about 45 minutes. Around 9:30 p.m., the night nurse arrived, and we would start to get him ready for bed. We had to give him his medicine, get him changed, brush his teeth, and put on splints and braces he sleeps with for his hands and feet. This process took an hour to an hour and a half as well. He needed to change positions about every four hours, so around 3:00

a.m., the night nurse turned him on his other side, and then again around 6:30 a.m., to his back. Then it was time to wake up and do it all over again. It was not very glamorous, but given the circumstances, I wouldn't have done it any differently.

I've always been very hands on with my children and John Michael wouldn't have wanted it any other way. So while others may do it differently or choose to utilize more help, John Michael and I chose to do it the way that made us the happiest. Our motto throughout this whole process has been, "It's not forever. It can't be." We hold on to this with great faith!

It was so great to be home, but it was so hard to be home. The adjustment was hard, and four years later, it is still hard. While we were away, my life stopped. My responsibilities stopped. Many things were put on hold. Once home, I wanted and needed my life back, but I couldn't have both. I couldn't be the mom I was at Shepherd and the mom I was normally at home. There wasn't enough time in a day. John Michael took up the majority of my day. Ben got the leftovers. Fortunately, Ryan was an adult and extremely self-sufficient, but she still wanted her mom at times. There were days when I don't even know how I survived.

I became angry. I was angry at the naysayers, angry at those who kept saying I couldn't keep doing this. I was angry at life. I was even angry at God. Why was He taking so long? We had people all over the world praying for John Michael. The Pope had even e-mailed him! Are you listening, God? Even though I questioned, my faith did not weaken. It was all I had to hang onto. This is what kept me going. The many prayers for me sustained me, made me stronger, and gave me a strength I didn't even know I had.

I was reminded of another story in the Bible of the death of Lazarus in John 11. Mary and Martha were so upset that it took Jesus so long to come and heal their brother. Even his disciples questioned him on why he waited. When Jesus finally arrived, they said to Him, "If you had only come sooner." I often feel that way – if only, why so long, what are you waiting for? But Jesus spoke these words to them, and I will rest in this because I believe!

"Then Jesus said to her, 'Your *son* will rise again.' Then Jesus said, 'Did I not tell you that if you believed, you would see the glory of God?'" – John 11:23, 40

The actual verse uses "brother." I inserted "son" instead.

This is what I cling to. This is what gets me out of bed every day. This is how I do it!

I was also convicted by this story because it says, "Jesus wept." Those two words are so beautiful to me. Jesus loves us enough to see our pain, to feel our pain, He even weeps for us.

I had an experience where I was listening to a speaker at our church and all of a sudden, I felt something warm on my face. I went to wipe it away, and I realized it was tears. Tears were flowing freely from my eyes, and I wasn't even aware that I was crying. I was in a crowded room with people I would never think of crying in front of. I tried to stop them from coming, but they still came.

The message was definitely something that resonated with me, but I would have never allowed myself to freely weep in public like that. To this day, I honestly feel those were not my tears, but the tears of Jesus. He was weeping for me. He knew the pain and struggle that I was feeling, and He openly wept for me that day.

I think we all have little moments like this where God is so present, so close, but often times we are too busy or too blind to recognize it's Him. John Michael's stroke has made me be more purposeful throughout my day, actively looking for God anywhere I can find Him. He is there. He is all around. I encourage you to stop, slow down, and really look. Before you know it, you too will be amazed to see that He is there every step of the way.

One of the strongest statements made to me during this time was from one of Rowly's cousins, a fellow Camp Ridgcrester who came to visit John Michael at the Shepherd Center.

As he was leaving, he thanked me for the privilege of visiting John Michael, and he said it was evident that the Holy Spirit was very present in the room. I had felt it since the PICU, so to have a young man experience it and confirm it was pretty amazing.

Chapter 53

The Beach

(Vickie)

In trying to keep things as normal as possible, and since it was summertime, we headed to our condo at the beach. It is a small condo, three bedroom and two baths, but there was no way to make it accessible. Fortunately, we had a ground floor unit with large sliding glass doors across the back. We used a portable ramp to get him in and out of the condo. Once he was inside, there really was no place to go. It was basically one large room with a living area and a kitchen. We had an extralarge island in the middle of the kitchen that served as our table with three barstools on each side. The master was in the back and there were two bedrooms and a small bath up front. Unfortunately, the complex did not have a ramp to get down to the beach, only stairs. We purchased a beach wheelchair that had large rubber wheels and was made out of PVC pipes. It actually floats.

I am still amazed how they have made so many things adaptable. The only way to get John Michael down to the beach was to roll him through the dunes. Of course, the dunes are protected and this is not legal, but it worked, and it was our only option. It took at least three strong men to get him down. Fortunately, we had owned our condo for 13 years at the time, and we knew almost everyone there. Someone was always around to help. We petitioned the board to build a ramp, but sadly, we were turned down. I still don't understand. The ramp would have benefited everyone. Many people rent to "snow-birds." I have seen them over the years. Some are too old or frail to go down the stairs to the beach, so they just sit by the pool. It would have been a huge help to the moms with several small children trying to carry beach toys, chairs, snacks, and so on because they cannot roll a cart or a wagon down the stairs.

Sometimes I feel like we did not try hard enough to get it passed, but we had no time or energy. It was too hard and too much work to go to the condo, so we ended up selling it and buying a new one down the road. While it is much larger, with room for John Michael to maneuver around, and they have a nice ramp to easily get down to the beach, it isn't the same. Now don't get me wrong, I do not see this as a major tragedy. I have way too many other things to call tragedies, but this hit hard emotionally. We loved our condo. It was our home away from home. So many memories were made there. We used to spend most of the summer there and just about every holiday except Christmas.

That summer would be our last 4th of July at that condo. Just like most towns, the 4th is heavily celebrated. The law states no fireworks are allowed on the beach. It also appears that no one adheres to that law. It is quite the show. All up and down the beach are major firework displays. It is almost like a tennis match to watch. With each loud boom we'd turn our heads to the right, then to the left. There was a rumor that some years the people to the left would have a competition with the people on the right and the displays were amazing! And so it would go on for a good hour.

Because it was so hard to get JM down to the beach, we just rolled up to the dunes and watched from there. Since we did not need to provide fireworks, I always bought sparklers. John Michael decided it would be funny to put a sparkler in his mouth and take a snap chat picture. Again, against my better judgement, I went along with it. Needless to say, it fell and burnt a hole in his shirt leaving a nice little scar on his stomach. He thought this was very funny. I, however, thought, "I told you so!" I guess he wanted another scar to match the one from his feeding tube.

CHAPTER 54

Our New Normal

(Vickie)

O ur new normal was anything but normal. Our new normal was hard and exhausting. Everything we did that we once used to do was twice as hard and did not bring near the joy or satisfaction. We love going to Tallahassee. Whether to see a football game, baseball game, or a lacrosse game, we rarely turned down a chance to go. So when football season came, we were off. This would be our first overnight trip since his stroke. I think I packed everything possible, and then some, to make sure we would have everything we needed. At this point, John Michael was still on the feeding tube and eating pureed food. I remember spending half of the day pureeing food for the weekend that I would just have to reheat.

We arrived in Tallahassee late Friday afternoon. Friday nights before a game are always extremely busy in Tallahassee, but we finally found a restaurant that could accommodate us.

Normally, we would have connected with friends and enjoyed the live music and fun up and down the street, but it was too crowded and maneuvering the wheelchair through the crowd was too much. By the time we finally got to bed it was probably midnight. We did not bring night help, so Mick and I were on duty. Even though John Michael only woke up twice, I woke up tired. Instead of going out for a fun breakfast, we ate in the room. It was just easier. It was game day, and while normally I would have been excited, this time I was not.

We have had season tickets for years in the stadium and have sat by the same families. They have watched my children grow up, and we are now watching their children have their own. We have celebrated many amazing victories and hugged through many excruciating defeats. But we would now have to sit in the Club section in the end zone in the back, handicap row. I knew these were first world problems, but it was just not the same. It was another reminder of how much our lives had changed.

We do not make it to games as often as we used to, and at the end of every season, I find myself hoping and praying that next fall things will be different. I'm still waiting.

We do venture out as much as we can. Typically, it is to a sporting event. It is so hard to see your once very active child limited to events and activities that are spectator sports. Life can be so cruel. No one wants to just be a spectator, certainly not an adventurous, risk-taking young man. So instead of dwelling on it, we strive to make his life as full as possible. We go to many local high school and college lacrosse games, Orlando Magic basketball games, Orlando City soccer games and have seen numerous shows and concerts at the Dr. Phillips Center for the Performing Arts. The best way we have found to make him feel more than just a spectator is to have him meet the performer or athlete. Since we have been home, he has met Brad Paisley, several Orlando Magic players, and Donald Trump!

During Donald Trump's campaign, friends of ours reached out to someone they knew on his campaign. We then received a call that Mr. Trump would like us to attend a rally he was having at the Sanford airport, which was just 20 minutes from our house. John Michael was very excited. We brought a JMStrong shirt with us, hoping to give it to him. As we waited for his plane to land, we heard people cheering for Trump, but then also began hearing chants of "JMStrong!" It was unbelievable. A group of people in the crowd recognized us and wanted to show their support. It was amazing.

Once Trump's plane arrived, he gave his speech and then was being hurried back to the plane. He was behind schedule and needed to get going. Now mind you, I did not know what to expect. The media has always made him out to be a not-so-nice kind of person. But the person I met that day was the complete opposite. On his way to re-board, he stopped to meet us, and we had a lovely conversation. He was very genuine. When we gave him the JMStrong shirt, he said, "Now this one, I'm keeping." It felt like he wanted to spend more time with us, but they made him say his goodbyes. He wished John Michael the best of luck, gave us a wave and was on his way; a very special day indeed, especially since he is now president. The President of the United States of America has a JMStrong shirt. Now that is pretty cool!

With John Michael's friends away at college, we were grateful that Rowly had deferred until the spring. They decided to take a class at the college down the road, Rollins College. John Michael was thinking he might like to be a real estate attorney, so they took a business law class. The course load was a bit much, so they took it as observers. What a great friend Rowly was for taking him to class each week.

Jared was at Florida State playing baseball, so we went to watch him play when we could. Jake decided to come home after his first semester, so when Rowly left for Pepperdine in January, Jake stepped in and was there for John Michael. While Rowly took John Michael to class, Jake took John Michael to The Porch. It was social time. The Porch is a Rollins College hangout. Jake even had the bartender name a shot "the JMStrong shot."

Even without his voice, John Michael has made new friends, mostly with the trainers and interns at CORE who are closer to him in age. They come over and hang out at the house, take him to movies, or come with us on some of our outings. I am so thankful for them. Matt has been friends with John Michael since we started at CORE. They became fast friends. Several of the other guys that he befriended have moved on and are no longer around.

Being the ladies' man that he is, he also has several girlfriends who like to come over and hang out. We love when Bianco visits and brings her "slutty brownies." They are delicious, cookie dough and Oreos covered in brownie batter and baked! They don't last very long. When they are not having "roomie night," Rachel and Nicole will come for dinner and hang out. Rachel has also been a huge help to me with John Michael, but most importantly, has been a great friend to him as well.

Not long after we were first home, Rowly's family sent Dr. Lisa Corsa to evaluate John Michael. Dr. Corsa has a physical therapy facility in Boca Raton called Premiere Therapy Solutions. When Dr. Corsa arrived, I was not prepared for her. While she is extremely smart and great at what she does, I was not ready for her take charge attitude. She had a lot to say about what we should and should not be doing. I was having none of it. So when she recommended that we go to her facility for a week, I politely said, "No, thank you."

She was very helpful in organizing and managing the therapists I had in place here at home, but at the time, that was all I could handle. Fast forward about a year later, and I was ready. John Michael was ready. We needed a change of scenery and a fresh set of eyes and opinions. So we headed to Premier Therapy Solutions for a week.

After the first couple of days, John Michael was ready to go. She was doing everything very differently from what he was used to. But on the third day it seemed to click, and he finally understood the madness to her method. I told John Michael that this was like his face-off drills for lacrosse. The coach breaks down the face-off into incremental steps and has them practice one step at a time before putting it all together. This is exactly what he was doing now, breaking down every movement into incremental steps before he can put it all together. At that point, he could activate and volitionally do the first three phases of gait. He was now beginning to activate the next step, lifting the knee and pulling the leg forward. He was looking forward to getting home and putting it into practice to make that true connection!

Dr. Lisa Corsa is an amazing physical therapist, but she also acts as our medical concierge. She organized a team of doctors

— neuroradiologists, neurologists, neurosu
erventionalists, and so on. She had them c
MRA, blood work, a swallow study, and a
again, we were taken by surprise with the results. We learned
that John Michael has a congenital anomaly in the brain
called vertebral basilar hypoplasia. He has low blood flow or
hypo-perfusion in the posterior circulation of the brain. There
are several arterial structures that have stenosis or narrowing.
The left basilar artery and several branches are narrower leading
to hypoperfusion or low blood flow. *Wow!* I wasn't prepared for
that.

Essentially, John Michael was born with very narrow basilar
arteries. He always had very low blood pressure. They feel that
being the athlete that he is and probable dehydration along
with his low flow, he stroked. They also think that possibly as
he grew and worked out harder, he required more blood flow
and the arteries were just not big enough to supply adequate
flow. What is interesting, however, is that the arteries traveling
from the front of the brain to the back are larger than normal,
thus providing him with sufficient blood flow to compensate
for the narrow ones. Isn't that just like God? He provides a way!

But what did this mean going forward? They completed an
ultrasound of the arteries to determine their size and flow. They
are the size of a coffee straw when they should be the size of a
normal straw! We hoped that stinting would be a possibility.

Operating on the brain stem is so risky, and with the arteries being so small, we were told it wasn't even a possibility. Going forward, we have to make sure he is well hydrated and constantly monitor his blood pressure as well as being on double platelet therapy. What John Michael has is extremely rare. Eighty percent of those with this condition do not even live! He is a true miracle. The doctors are amazed that he survived and amazed that he was ever able to play sports at the level at which he played.

It took me a while to wrap my brain around all of this. It was a lot of information to process. I had to relive the nightmare of December 2015 too many times during that month. It was hard to stay focused and not let those thoughts and memories overtake me. I had to rely on my faith to keep me strong. We were grateful to know the "why," especially since we were initially told we would never know. No one could have seen this coming, but so much makes sense now. The episodes of light-headedness and almost fainting several times throughout his childhood were all leading up to that moment. The doctors back then said it was probably dehydration, which it was, but it was slowing the blood flow to his brain and we never knew. Life is crazy, but God is good, and the larger arteries sustained him for almost 18 years.

We did get some good news from all of those tests. While we were initially told the whole pons was destroyed by his stroke, we learned that 30% of the pons is still intact! This was huge news. This is why they feel he is progressing. They also agreed he is no longer considered locked-in! John Michael loved hearing this great news! The progress he has made thus far amazed them, and they were very positive and hopeful of his recovery. But like we already knew, it was going to be a slow recovery.

CHAPTER 55

Our First Thanksgiving

(Vickie)

Our first Thanksgiving home in 2016, we spent it as we normally do, at our beach condo. I was so excited because John Michael was actually going to get to eat most of the food. The tube had been out for a few weeks now and he was eating a soft food and pureed diet, which of course meant he would get to eat Grandma's mashed potatoes. I love to cook, but somehow, I have never mastered the art of making mashed potatoes, so Grandma always had the honor of making them. It has always been my kids' favorite side dish. After not having eaten them for almost a year, he was ready to dig in.

The following year, we decided to mix it up a bit and head to the mountains for Thanksgiving. We made the 10-hour drive to Highlands, North Carolina to meet our good friends, the Torris family. We rented a beautiful home at the top of the mountain. John Michael's camp friend Connor came up and spent the holiday with us. My motto that year was, "I am not cooking." I was exhausted from taking care of John Michael, and I had hosted Thanksgiving since I can remember and was ready for a break. We had a wonderful time shopping on the main street and eating at our favorite restaurants. This Thanksgiving was even more exciting than the last because John Michael was on a regular diet, which meant he would be eating everything just as it was prepared! Huge gains indeed.

One morning we decided to go on one of our favorite hikes. It was a long, wide path that was not very steep. We had brought John Michael's beach chair so he could go as well. Well, this took a team effort, but we made it up the mountain! Connor, once again, took friendship and not leaving your friend behind to another level. It was no easy feat. There were times when we pushed going forward and times when we pulled him backwards. While it wasn't a steep mountain, it was a long, slow incline. The path was uneven at times paved with tree roots, fallen branches and rocky at times. I think we all took an Advil when we got back.

But of course, it was well worth it. John Michael felt so great being at the top of that mountain. He had been hiking that same mountain since he could walk. Actually, before he could walk, Mick would carry him up in a backpack! At the time, we stood him up and took some great photos. To the unknowing person, it looked as if everything was normal. But if pictures could talk, it would've told you how exhausted we were and how we felt anything but normal.

We lingered a while at the top, maybe because we wanted to pretend for a little longer that everything was normal. The ride down was much quicker and easier. Gravity helped, of course.

Since the next day was Thanksgiving, I was getting very excited to be served. We had reservations at the local Inn. While we were in town, a local asked where we would be dining, and when we told them, they politely said, "You do know it's a pre-fixed menu."

We had a few picky eaters in our group, so we decided to check it out. The menu looked like most would enjoy it, but then we noticed the price. My little guy, Ben, would not eat enough food to amount to paying that price in a month's time! Our friends agreed that no one wanted to spend that kind of money, so we bailed. We went to the local market and the butcher said he had one fresh turkey left in the back. We took it and grabbed whatever sides we could find.

I ended up cooking that year. We took pictures and called it "the meal we weren't supposed to cook." The meal ended up being pretty good for being thrown together in a few hours. John Michael thoroughly enjoyed every bite. It was a much-needed break from the daily routine that was getting much too monotonous. The time with our friends was very special. It was a Thanksgiving I think we will all remember for years to come.

CHAPTER 56

The Test

(John Michael)

At Camp Ridgecrest, when you pass the Little Chief test, you are given an Indian name. I passed on my second try in 2013. I was given the name Acclaimed Collie! A collie is, of course, a type of dog with long flowing hair. It was perfect. My friend Connor from Myrtle Beach had the honor of being "tapped out" for the test at age 12, the youngest age possible. He never could quite keep his mouth shut, which was ironic because he was so quiet when I met him. There was one time when he talked with only three hours left!

Like my mom said, it's basically an 18-hour test that starts at midnight and you can't talk. During the test, they tell you that you can't talk to anyone, so talk to God. It is not only a test of physical and mental strength, but of faith. I never thought this would literally be the case.

The year I passed the test it was Connor's fourth time around. We both made it to the final portion of the test, and we all thought for sure this was God's plan to have us pass together, right? Connor accidentally answered someone out loud with 45 minutes left...

Needless to say, everyone was devastated. The next year would be his fifth and final try at the test. He would pass easily and be given the name Relentless Nighthawk.

In the summer of 2017, we drove to North Carolina to pick up my younger brother Ben from camp and Connor met us there! At Camp Ridgecrest, it is a tradition that at the closing ceremony the new Little Chiefs (if any) are named and then have the opportunity to introduce themselves in front of everyone, along with those in attendance who have previously passed the test. I was hesitant, obviously, to do it as probably the only person who's been up there in a chair, certainly the only one remotely close to my age. Connor and I decided to do it together and he would introduce me. Connor said who I was and my Little Chief name and there was a round of applause. It also happened to be my dad's birthday, so I had him announce happy birthday to him. Connor currently goes to The Citadel, and to this day still comes down whenever he can throughout the year.

"Consider it pure joy, my brothers and sisters, whenever you face trials of many kinds, because you know that the testing of your faith produces perseverance. Let perseverance finish its work so that you may be mature and complete, not lacking anything." – James 1:2-4

CHAPTER 57

Running

(Vickie)

Oh, how I miss the peaceful, predictable routine of life. It has since been replaced by uncertainty and sometimes fear. I'm so very tired, not just physically tired, but emotionally exhausted. I am tired of this disappointment lingering a little too long and being a bit too hard. It's the kind of exhaustion that causes paralysis. I sometimes have moments when I physically cannot do something. I want to make those calls, run those errands, or even go for a run. But it's like I'm frozen, unable to move. Maybe it is God telling me to rest.

The first time I went for a run was back when John Michael was in the PICU. It was a couple of weeks later and I was pretty much forced to go. I did not want to go; I had never been so exhausted in my life. Everyone knows how much I love to run, so they thought it would be good for me. So I went for a run. I remember my legs feeling like heavy bricks. I could hardly move them. And then something happened: I honestly felt like

God was picking up my legs one at a time and moving them for me. It was the craziest feeling, and I will never forget it. It turned out that the run was good for me. It did make me feel better, but it took a long time to be able to run without being emotionally drained and sobbing at the end.

I learned that when I am weak emotionally, I compensate with my physical strength. So when I would deplete myself physically like on a run, I could not contain my emotions. The tears would just come the moment I stopped running, sometimes even mid-run. I've learned to let the tears flow and to stop trying to be so strong all the time. Allowing myself to feel the pain was the first step toward healing the pain. The longer I avoided my emotions by stuffing them somewhere deep within, the longer I delayed true healing. I could numb it with a bottle of wine or ignore it by acting brave and confident, but I couldn't pretend it didn't exist. It eventually caught up with me, and by not dealing with my pain, my body suffered the consequences.

I didn't have a clue as to what I was doing or how this was all going to work out, and it scared me to death. But you don't know what you don't know, and I was in survival mode. I stuffed my feelings deep down inside of me, mostly because I did not have the time or the energy to deal with how I felt and how all of this was affecting me. I think I also did it to please others, to not disappoint others. I had it all together on the outside, while inside all of the stress and trauma was literally eating at my body.

I read recently that you have to train your mind to be stronger than your emotions or else you'll lose yourself every time. I used to agree with this statement. You shouldn't let your emotions trump the truth. But what happens when your truth is so bad, so raw, that you can no longer control your emotions? I think I had trained my brain so well to control my emotions that I never stopped to really feel, to really experience what I was going through. When my truth became too much to bear, I had a hard time controlling my emotions. I guess what I'm trying to say is by trying to be stronger than my emotions, I began to suffer from PTSD. I have never properly dealt with all the traumatic things that have happened over the last three years, but after I was diagnosed with cancer, I collapsed under the weight of being too strong.

CHAPTER 58

A Downward Spiral

(Vickie)

Two years after John Michael's stroke, I was diagnosed with Stage 1 breast cancer, like I didn't already have enough on my plate. November 2017 started a major downward spiral. I went for my yearly mammogram which, thank goodness, I have been very faithful in doing. In early December, I received a letter stating I needed to return to get a better image of areas of concern. I thought, "Hmm, no big deal. It happens to many. It could just be dense breast tissue or calcifications. No big deal, right?"

On December 21ˢᵗ, I went in for a higher quality mammogram.

"Sorry, we need to do an ultrasound."

"Sorry, we are going to have to biopsy two areas."

Wait what? To this day, I feel so bad for the poor young man who gave me the news. He made the mistake of asking if I was okay. At this point, with Christmas around the corner, and it just having been the two-year anniversary of John Michael's stroke, I lost it. He was so sweet trying to comfort me about the biopsy, but I started to almost laugh and had to say, "You have no idea!"

Fast forward to early January (I couldn't get in any earlier due to the holidays) and I had my biopsy. Great news! It was LCIS – lobular carcinoma in situ – non-cancerous, but could potentially become cancerous. I would need a lumpectomy and I would be good to go. I went for an MRI to confirm the areas of concern and, just my luck, they found a third area, and it was time for biopsy number two. It was now February, and I was in DC helping Ryan move when I got the call.

"I am so sorry, but it is Stage 1."

Wait, what?

On March 9th, I underwent a double mastectomy (it was only in my left breast, but I chose to do a double). They also removed my lymph nodes. The great news – I am cancer-free! It has not spread, and they got it all! The even better news is that my BRCA was clean, meaning I do not carry the breast cancer or ovarian cancer gene.

Praise God my daughter and sisters do not have to worry. I'm good to go, except now they run a test called a MammaPrint on the actual tumor to determine the probability of recurrence. Well, wouldn't you know? I'm cancer-free, but the tumor carried an abnormal gene that puts me at a high risk of recurrence. I would have to have four rounds of chemotherapy.

Wait, what?

Although I was in the high-risk range, I was on the very low end of the range. Having the four treatments would give me a 95% chance of non-recurrence. I had no choice.

I'm not going to lie. Chemo is evil! I feel I did very well, but it was not easy. When I started my treatments, I decided to use the Dignicap. It is a cold cap that you wear before, during, and after treatment, making my treatment last six hours! It causes hypothermia to the hair follicles in hopes of minimal hair loss. I had to drive to Tampa from Orlando for treatment because they did not have the Dignicap available in Orlando at the time. Unfortunately, it did not work so well for me. After two treatments, I had lost almost 60% of my hair. I had to wear a wig or a cap anyway, so I decided to stop the Dignicap and complete my last two treatments here in Winter Park. My treatments were only three hours!

I am once again humbled by this experience. I have found myself in the book of Job quite often during these past two years. I often joke that I feel a bit like him. Life is not fair. I've tried to teach my kids this since they were little, but that doesn't make it any easier. I continue to try to be like Job when he said to his wife, "Shall we accept good from God and not trouble?"

I certainly had a lot of good in my life! Once again, I found myself relying on my "tribe." I could not have gotten through this without them – rides to chemo, every text, call, card, meal, visit, help with Ben, and so on. I will always count my blessings, and they are definitely big ones. God has, indeed, tested me throughout these trials. My hope and prayer is that I have served Him well and continue to do so.

The day of my last treatment I wore my JMStrong shirt and I rang the bell. I rang it in gratitude that I had beaten cancer, and I rang it in hopes that very soon, John Michael would be ringing his own kind of bell that he has completely beaten locked-in syndrome!

CHAPTER 59

Moses and Joshua

(Vickie)

My friend Christine gave me the sweetest analogy of my situation. It is the example of Moses from Exodus 17 when Joshua and the Israelites went to battle. As long as Moses kept his arms lifted, they had success, but the moment he let them down, they would begin to lose. Eventually, Moses had to have people help hold up his arms when he was too tired and could no longer hold them up alone.

John Michael is Joshua. He is the one fighting the battle, doing the hard work. I am like Moses, standing above, watching, keeping my arms outstretched in prayer, doing all the behind-the-scenes hard work of taking care of John Michael. I, too, have become too fatigued at times. When I am tired and have no energy to be positive or to even pray, this can affect John Michael's attitude as well and we all start to lose.

I am grateful for the many that hold up my arms for me, lifting me up in prayer, giving me rest so John Michael can keep fighting his battle and have success. This experience has taken the saying "it takes a village" to a whole new level. On my weakest days, when I just can't, when I just don't want to, I have an army of people lifting me up in prayer, and this is what gives me the strength to press on to help John Michael in any way I can to get his life back – the life he misses, the life I miss for him, and for myself.

I am reminded of a worship service we heard while at the Shepherd Center. We are called to be a light in this world. We hide our light behind fear and doubt. These are feelings my family has experienced. I was comforted by the thought that doubt isn't lack of faith, it's simply a crisis of faith that ultimately leads to a strengthened faith. While all of my friends, family, and even complete strangers have been such incredible light to us, places like Shepherd and CORE bring strangers together to be light for each other.

We hold fast to the fact that the light of Christ shines more brightly in our weakness. We help each other to shine our light and have courage, faith, and love instead. We have courage because we are strong enough with God. We have faith because we trust and have seen prayers answered, and we have love because He first loved us. We all walk around with wounds – even when John Michael is restored to perfect health, the wounds from this will always be there. But as the chaplain said, "Jesus carried his wounds around and we will carry ours, but they do not own us. We cannot let them define us. But we are to show them to the doubting Thomases of this world." And by doing this, we will be His light to this world, and we will see that our suffering has purpose.

If I've heard it once, I've heard it a million times, and years ago, I probably uttered these same words. I have come to hate the saying, "God only gives you what you can handle." Honestly, if I hear it one more time, I might hit somebody. This is not a Biblical statement. Anyone who has been hit square in the face with a tragedy will agree that they cannot handle the situation on their own. Then pile trial upon trial, sorrow upon sorrow, and there is no way on this side of heaven that anyone can handle it alone.

It is but for the grace of God that I am standing today. There is nothing in my flesh that is capable of handling what I have been through. The good Lord has equipped me to handle it. He has given me the strength, the attitude, and the desire to rise above and do whatever it takes to get through.

Trust me, I do not always choose to use the things He has equipped me with, and it is on those days that self-pity, doubt, and fear control my emotions. It would be very easy for me to say, "I'm not getting out of bed today. I am worn out and I just can't do it anymore." But every day, I choose to listen to God, obey Him, and do what He has called me to do. At this time, He has called me to care for my son. I think God equips everyone, but you have to choose whether you are going to use the things He has given you, whether you will be controlled by your negative emotions, or whether you believe the world when it tells you, "It's okay to feel that way. You deserve to feel that way. You've been through a lot." While that may be true, you cannot linger with those feelings. Clinging to those negative feelings leads to depression. I've learned that you must acknowledge them, feel them for a short period, then release them to God.

CHAPTER 60

Seashells

(Vickie)

The beach is one of my most favorite places – my happy place, as I call it. My counselor taught me to go there in my mind when these feelings tend to linger. These feelings are not allowed there. I took it to another level.

On my last trip to the beach, I collected a seashell for every negative feeling and emotion I have felt. Each shell was different. Some were dark in color and some were broken and worn, just like me. The worse shape it was in, the more negative emotion I attached to it.

After collecting them, I walked along the shore and released them, one at a time. I thought about the feeling and how it had impacted me, and as I tossed it back into the ocean, I gave it to God. It's His now. Don't get me wrong, it's not like I will never have those same feelings again, but now I take comfort that God has this, and maybe the next time I go to the beach

I will collect shells that are bright in color and in better condition and name them as my blessings. But this time, I will keep them.

People think just because you are a Christian and have faith, you should not worry. Another phrase I constantly hear is, "You are so strong." Actually, I am not. If I want to be of help to John Michael, be a mother to my two other kids, a wife, a friend, and a daughter, I have no choice but to be strong. Worry is often thought of as a sin because we are not relying on or trusting in God. But worry is a natural human reaction. It's when we wallow in it and let it control us that we fail to put our full trust in Him. We need to own our pain, our trials, claim it, acknowledge and name it, then give it to God, and He will carry us and sustain us and always provide a way out. Even if our circumstances do not change, we can be changed, our attitude can change, our perspective can change.

The Bible says God will sustain us, carry us through the good times and bad. But sustaining is not the same as delivering, and oh, how I desperately want John Michael delivered from this. What if He only sustains him, but never delivers him? I really struggle with this. This is my greatest fear. But just maybe, we need to be sustained before He delivers us, because if He delivered us right away, we would have never learned to fully rely on Him. And maybe His deliverance looks nothing like what I think it should. So for now, I thank Him for sustaining us and wait and pray that my hope of deliverance, John Michael's complete restoration, will be His, and even if it is not the same, I will learn to accept it.

Even if – the hardest two words to say and truly mean them. Some days I feel like I truly mean it; there are other days when I say it, but don't really mean it; and some days I can't even say them at all. How could God leave him like this? Why would a kind, compassionate loving God not restore him? Those are two very small words with such a big meaning. I've wanted to write them in my updates for some time now, but I struggled with really meaning them. I've borrowed them from a song by Mercy Me. The refrain says: "I know You're able and I know You can / Save through the fire with Your mighty hand / But even if You don't / My hope is You alone."

I think I'm getting closer to really meaning it. I think by finally putting it out there, maybe now I'll feel some account-ability to try my hardest to mean it. I know He is able. I know He can. My hope has always been that He will. I know John Michael will be healed and restored to fullness one day in heaven, but oh, how I want it in his lifetime. No matter what, I am called to trust. I'm called to trust that even if He doesn't, He is still faithful and He has a greater plan for John Michael, greater than anything I could ever imagine. For us, obviously the true victory is John Michael restored, walking, talking, and functioning independently as he used to, but I have to accept that maybe the victory isn't all about John Michael being restored. Maybe it's about how we handle the journey. Am I going to let my disappointments and challenges control me? Or am I going to get up every day and face it head on, relying on God for strength and looking for His goodness throughout the day? It's not easy. I have to wake up and remind myself to pray for the courage to trust Him and say with confidence, "Lord, even if You don't."

For now, I have claimed this verse for John Michael, and I cling to this promise (I inserted John Michael's name): "Nevertheless, I will bring health and healing to John Michael: I will heal him and will let him enjoy abundant peace and security. I will bring John Michael back from captivity and rebuild him as he was before." Jeremiah 33:6-7

CHAPTER 61

Precious Children

(Vickie)

I write this very tenderly, because unfortunately, I know a few too many people who have lost precious children. Honestly, on my hardest, weakest days, I am reminded of them and I turn my pity to gratitude that my son is alive. Many may not understand this and may actually think I am pretty awful for feeling this way because I can still give my son a hug and tell him how much I love him. But after meeting so many people at the Shepherd Center and at CORE in similar situations as myself, I don't think people understand that we have to grieve as well.

I am by no means comparing the two situations. The grief you feel for a child you lost is very different from grieving your living child. I hope to never know that kind of grief. What I do know is that I stare grief in the face every day. Grieving a living child is indescribable. It cannot be dismissed or denied. While you are so happy your child is still with you, you miss who they once were, what they once could do, what they were supposed to be doing and becoming. To watch your child lose everything is devastating. Every day I wake up and beg God to give him something, anything, back.

I miss my son. I miss how he used to always tell me "thank you" after every meal I made for him. I miss his hugs. I miss yelling at him for driving too fast. I miss watching him play lacrosse. I miss how he always used to leave his dresser drawers open. I miss that he didn't get to go off to college. The list could go on. Ryan and Ben miss their brother and his friends miss him, too. I am grateful every day that he survived, that he is 100% cognitive, that he was always able to breathe on his own, that he is off the feeding tube and that he still continues to progress. But I had to learn how to allow myself to grieve him and not feel guilty. I lost a big part of my son, a big part of me. I still struggle with grieving my living child.

As I learn to accept what has been thrown upon us, it doesn't get any easier with time. Actually, the more time that passes, the bigger my grief becomes for all he continues to miss out on, for all the experiences he should be having, but cannot. Time is not my great healer as it is for most people facing grief.

CHAPTER 62

Determination

(Vickie)

We are now approaching almost four years post-stroke. When I look back over those years, I am amazed at all I have endured, all John Michael has had to endure, and all my family has endured. It's honestly overwhelming. I would have never thought we would still be where we are with so far to go. I can now see how I have been in complete survival mode. It's hard to describe. You can't realize it until you reflect back, and that takes time. Last year I would not have been able to say that, of course, because last year I was going through chemo.

I've been told I suffer from PTSD. No one should be surprised. How does one handle your child suffering a devastating stroke, leaving him with no independent function, your family dog dies, you get breast cancer, your mom dies, and the day-to-day stress and the million other things in between? I want to say it gets easier, I want to say I've made it this far as gracefully as most think, but I'd be lying. It is so much harder now. But during this time, when most would look at all that has happened and how hard my life still is, one would think I would feel as if God had deserted me.

I am often asked how I still have such faith. It's like that day at the Shepherd Center: if I stop and truly look around, God is everywhere in my life. He never abandons me or forsakes me. Trust me, I have had moments of feeling like He has, but those moments are when I must make a conscience effort to stop so I can see His hand in my life.

I see the three amazing children He gave me. I can see how He spared John Michael's life and is using his story to inspire and motivate people. I see how much progress John Michael has made and continues to make. I see how he delivered me from breast cancer by catching it early and through chemotherapy. I see how He has changed me by deepening my faith and calling me to show others that my faith is my foundation. Without it I would crumble.

Life is hard under the best circumstances. I used to tell my kids, "You are one bad choice away from ruining your life." But sometimes our life gets ruined by things that are not our choice or are out of our control. In reality, everyone is one moment away from having their lives changed forever, for better or for worse.

John Michael still has therapy five days a week for three to four hours a day. He is now able to drink out of a straw, and we no longer use the letter board. He is speaking! It is very quiet and most of the time I am lip reading, but he is speaking. Praise God! We have purchased numerous devices and gadgets over these last few years. Some are a success while others are a waste of money. And some he just hasn't been ready for. He uses small buttons on a couple of fingers that he has good movement with, and he can now text with those fingers instead of the head array on his chair. We have a mobile arm support that he is using to help self-feed. His core has become much stronger, and he is working hard on strengthening the deep core muscles that will help with his balance while sitting and standing. He continues to make progress, even though it feels like a snail's pace. This progress helps to keeps us going. As long as he is progressing, there is always hope of more to come.

Most days, he does it with a smile on his face and a great attitude. But he is only human, after all, and he definitely has had his moments. I could count on one hand how many times he has truly broken down and cried about his situation. God has certainly equipped him with an attitude of acceptance and determination that is incredible to watch.

CHAPTER 63

A Day in My Life

(John Michael)

A typical day for me begins when I wake up around 7:45. Two nurses lift me out of bed with a Hoyer (because I am undressed with a towel over me) into a plastic shower chair and help me go to the bathroom and shower. At our house right now, we added a bathroom onto our garage outside because the only bathroom downstairs isn't big enough. After that, I am Hoyered (because again, no clothes and now wet) onto a mat in the garage to get dried off and dressed. Then someone helps me stand up to get in my chair. My mom gives me breakfast and brushes my teeth. For some reason I'm very particular about who does what, like feed me or give me drinks, etc. Then, of course, my hair. Can't forget the hair.

Typically, I either have speech therapy from 9:00 to 10:00 with Shannon or I leave in the van at 9:30 for CORE. Of the many, many things people take for granted, certainly one is hopping in the car and just going. It's not that simple. First you have to deploy the ramp and drive me in, then I either lock in up front or sit in the back with my chair strapped down to the floor. At 6'2" (yes, I grew after the stroke), there aren't many vans I can easily get in and out and maneuver around inside from my chair. After I give the interior of the van some nice new touch-ups and lock in (which can take a few tries), then you can retract the ramp and close the door. The car won't let you put it in drive until everything is closed, which takes a good minute. Everything is, of course, automatic, but man is it fun when technology doesn't work and someone has to manually crank the ramp in and out.

At CORE, I have occupational therapy with Doro from 10-11 and training from 11-1. In occupational therapy I work on my upper extremities, mainly wrist, fingers, and biceps, with the ultimate goal of self feeding. At CORE, no one is technically a neuro PT, but they all have backgrounds in exercise science.

I've had many trainers during my time at CORE, but the ones who have been with me since day one are Matt Icenogle, Katie Yergler, and Bianca Saragusti. We work on everything including sitting, kneeling, standing, rolling, and walking. People think because I do therapy in a "gym" that it's similar to working out, but it's not at all. This bothers me because in my mind working out is fun. It's lifting weights and doing push-ups, pull-ups, sit-ups, etc. I need assistance for almost everything. I have to literally think about each individual movement while controlling my spasticity. It's as much or more of a mental workout than a physical one. What I do is, without a doubt, so much harder. After three total hours there, then I head home. Shortly after I get home, my mom gives me lunch, and I have speech with Shannon until the end of the day.

On the days that I start off with speech in the morning, I then have therapy at the house with my PT, Stacey, and my OT, Jen, from 10:00 to noon. We work out in the garage on a mat table doing prone on elbows or sitting at the edge. We also work on standing, with a table for my arms and a harness to help hold me up. After that, my mom gives me lunch and we head out around 1:20 to go to a place called Regenerative PT in Lake Nona. I'm there from 2:00 to 3:00 p.m. using their Redcord. Basically, I lay on a table that raises and lowers, and it's an overhead system with "red cords" hanging down from it. The cords attach to slings that go around different parts of my body. In theory, I could and have had my entire body suspended. Having my muscles in the air takes gravity out of the equation so I can move more freely.

We do a variety of exercises from my neck down to my feet, as well as prone and kneeling. I get home close to 4:00, and the therapy part of my day is finally over. However, just because that part of my day is over doesn't mean I'm done working. Over the years I've spent hours upon hours just practicing speech by myself. I also have the mobile arm supports that eliminate gravity so I can practice self-feeding. Besides the obvious, almost everything is harder for me. It was especially difficult in the beginning. For example, eating used to take easily three times longer than normal. When I was trying to get off the feeding tube there might have actually been a point where I was burning more calories than I was taking in (even though I was being fed)! I still typically cough (involuntarily to protect my airway) maybe once a meal. When I cough though, it is a full muscle contraction of my core which usually sends my whole body flying forward/legs kicking out! It's the same with my sneezes. They are a force to be reckoned with.

Occasionally I may get in bed and take a nap or have a massage or acupuncture. Other days my friends will come over. Jake, Jared, and Rachel are certainly the ones I hang out with the most. A big reason for that is because they are local. Jake and Jared currently live together in a house a couple of miles away. Rachel currently lives in an apartment in Altamonte Springs (close to CORE) with her roommate Nicole, who also works there.

Jake went to Mississippi State for a semester but decided it wasn't for him. He came home to eventually start his own tree service/land clearing/excavation company! He has been by my side ever since, arguably more than anybody who isn't a blood relative.

Jared obviously went to Florida State for baseball and did pretty well, but in the summer of 2018, decided to come home to Rollins College! This was huge because he would be around and I could actually go to his games because our house is practically on campus.

I actually met Rachel at CORE in 2017. Just a couple of days older than Ryan, she is from Massachusetts but ended up at the University of Central Florida. We became close friends right away.

I am beyond thankful for those three.

When my day is over, I usually stay up for a bit watching a show or on my phone. I can control the TV and lights with an app on my phone so my mom usually goes to bed earlier. The night nurse gets here at 9:30 on the weekdays, and I usually go to bed in the 11:00 hour range, meaning anywhere between 10 and 1. When I'm ready, the night nurse will hoyer me into bed because she can't stand me up by herself. She has to help turn me if I get uncomfortable throughout the night.

The majority of my friends are in school or graduated and working. I can't tell you how hard it is sitting at home while everybody else enjoys the "best four years of their lives," and I am pretty much no longer independent through no fault of my own whatsoever. It is maddening watching everyone (on social media or in public) completely oblivious (as I'm sure I was) to the fact that there's a whole other world out there.

I'm not going to lie to you. I get so frustrated sometimes – frustrated because I did nothing, absolutely nothing. I wasn't involved in an accident. I wasn't seriously injured physically. I was sitting in class doing nothing. But you know what? I have *something*. I have faith. I have hope. I have the promise of God's word. I am surrounded by people who love and care about me. I have family and friends who would literally do anything for me. My sister Ryan told me from the beginning in the PICU that God gives the toughest battles to his strongest warriors. I may not have everything I want anymore, but He certainly has given me everything I need, so I will continue to praise Him.

CHAPTER 64

Communicating

(John Michael)

Roughly about ten months I went without my phone. We tried at Shepherd and at home to use the Tobii with eye gaze, but it gave me a headache and was never completely accurate like I wanted, especially if it wasn't placed exactly right. I realize there are all kinds of technologies that will allow me to type and then say things aloud, but I was never fond of that idea, and I honestly just wanted to look at the layout on my actual phone.

In the fall of 2016, after searching high and low, we finally found this adapter, if you will, that plugs into my phone and worked by using switch control, which is universal on every iPhone under accessibility in Settings. These switches were placed on either side of my head on the head array with Velcro. At first, we had large red and yellow buttons for switches. We joked that I looked like a clown. Quickly, we got smaller, less conspicuous black ones.

The problem then became that I couldn't use my chair when I was on my phone, so every time I wanted to move or adjust my position, we would have to take everything off. We also went through several of the adapters because they weren't very reliable.

Wouldn't you know it? After a few months, we discovered something called an iDevice that connects the head switches that are already on my power chair to my phone through Bluetooth. No more wires!

I gained some finger motion after going to a place called the Brain Plasticity Center here in Orlando in 2017. We, of course, wanted to figure out how I could leverage this to use my phone. My occupational therapist, Doro, worked relentlessly at this. She fashioned different splints and even made a contraption using copper tape! It worked, but ultimately it was too finicky and hard to get in just the right spot.

Then we discovered the NeuroNode. It worked instantly. The NeuroNode is a small battery-powered sensor (kind of shaped like a dome) that can be placed practically anywhere to detect even the slightest movement. It goes on my hand with a replaceable sticky pad. The NeuroNode has many functions such as controlling the lights and TV, but I have an app on my phone that allows me to do that anyway. So I just use it with my phone. Traditionally, and technically, you only need one NeuroNode to use the phone, but I was so used to using two switches that it was just easier and faster for me to have two, both on my hand. I use them pretty much every day, sometimes more than once.

So there's your answer to "How does he text?" I use either the head array on my chair or the NeuroNodes using switch control. It's how I wrote everything in this book.

Chapter 65

I Will Walk Again

(John Michael)

I t's crazy how time went by so slow in the PICU and at Shepherd, but now, days just fly by. Pages seemingly fall off the calendar. Let me preface what I am about to say by telling you it is *not* meant to make you feel sorry for me at all. I'm just trying to help you understand exactly what it is that I deal with every single day. Trust me, I know there are those out there who have it worse and my heart goes out to them. Believe me when I say they are *always* in my thoughts and prayers.

I am currently 21 years old while I am writing this. People reading this are probably thinking, "Wow, this young man has some incredible faith." And you're right, or at least I'd like to think so. Before all this I was religious. I believed in God, went to church and all that, but my faith has increased dramatically over the years following the stroke. You might be wondering, "Why? Aren't you mad at God for doing this to you?" The answer is, "No." See, God doesn't do things to us, but *for* us. This is an opportunity, not a loss. That is a really, really, really hard pill for me to swallow, but there is nothing like extreme adversity to drive you straight into the arms of the Lord. At the end of the day though, I'm only human, and in the grand scheme of things I'm just a kid. At least I was when this happened to me. I was 17. Let me say that again... *seventeen*. My brain hasn't even fully developed!

College? What's that? I have never even lived on my own yet.

Working out and playing lacrosse, pretty much my favorite things to do—gone in the blink of an eye.

Take a second and imagine your almost-18-year-old self to your (now) almost-22-year-old self. Those were good times, right? Not for me.

I'm in a wheelchair, living at home with my mom (God love her, and I am so very blessed beyond all measure to have her). I can't even feed myself, let alone just leave and go where I want to go anymore. I can speak, but can't just converse with someone, especially if they are unfamiliar with how I sound, my breathing pattern, or the limited movement of my mouth and tongue. Basically all my independence is gone.

One thing I forgot to mention began at Shepherd. It is my clonus. Clonus is a series of involuntary rhythmic muscle contractions and relaxations. It is a result of certain neurological conditions and typically associated with spasticity. These large, violent motions (the opposite of a fasciculation or random small twitches) are caused by a reflex. Several primitive reflexes (ones we are born with but outgrow) are reintegrated after a brain stem injury because the signals that travel from the brain to the nerves telling the muscles to move are obviously damaged. It started in just my foot when it was dorsiflexed (stretched with the toes pulled upward so the calf/Achilles tendon is elongated), and it would cause my foot to move up and down in an uncontrollable rhythmic tapping motion.

I have sometimes experienced a full body reaction. Basically this means my entire body is shaking. People who are unfamiliar with me may think I'm having a seizure or something. I have never had (thank God) nor do I get seizures! Another thing people wonder about is my pain. Obviously, I feel pain (I've always had complete sensation everywhere) but since the PICU I have not been in any physical pain. Anyway, when it happens, my body is in an extensor synergy pattern, and the muscles don't know what to do or when to fire. Instead, everything goes together, all at once, into extension. Muscles can become locked out and very difficult to move. This tightness or "tone" can occur for a multitude of reasons from temperature change (especially cold) to my body being out of alignment when moving (especially quick movements) to emotional reasons (especially excitement or nervousness). I think everyone feels a little more tight and rigid in cold weather, but this is a whole other level.

My body, and even my taste buds, have also become overly sensitive to temperature. This means it's fairly easy for me to be affected by these changes in some way. Even though I do have head control, it can still be hard to hold up at times; a lot of this has to do with the weakness in my core. The position of my head is paramount when it comes to tone and spasticity. It's crazy how literally one little change or movement in position can completely throw me off or inhibit my ability to do things.

My emotions are probably about half the reason for my tone sometimes. Did I mention that I've had trouble controlling them, too? It was especially difficult in the beginning; I would laugh uncontrollably or at inappropriate times. This is common in brain injuries, to laugh or cry involuntarily. It will also kick in when I get excited or nervous, like when I meet someone of high stature or am put in a situation where I'm the center of attention. Sometimes it happens just from simply trying to converse or take a picture. Many times it gets to be too much to think about, and it is really hard to explain how extremely frustrating this can be. When I get clonus, most of the time, it will recede on its own. However, if it's more intense, it can be stopped through either pressure or unweighting of the limb. So that's one more thing I've had to deal with.

To this day I spend a lot of time thinking about what my life would be like right now and how this could have been prevented which probably isn't the best thing for me. I know there's the whole dehydration theory, but I don't buy that for a second. I know my body. If it was caused by dehydration, then it would've happened on the field, not sitting in the classroom! In the end, though, the fact is that it did happen. No matter what, things are going to happen in life that do not go your way. It's how you respond that matters.

I've learned a lot these past couple of years, a lot more than I cared to or thought I ever would know about some stuff. I do know that, no matter what, I will walk again. I'm tired of being afraid of being wrong, so I'm claiming it. It can't end like this. I've come too far and suffered through too much for anyone to tell me otherwise. I don't know when or how, but I've realized that doesn't matter because I know *who*. Only God can fully restore me.

Thoughts from our good friend, Scott Levitt

On Dec 13th, 2015, my wife and children and I were close longtime family friends of the Nights. Just one day later, everything changed. I went from a family friend to a family health advocate during what was rapidly becoming a horrifying event for our good friend's family.

When I arrived at the hospital on the night of Dec 14th, it became brutally apparent to me that the Nights were in no position to be able to rationally deal with what was happening to their son. The confusion, the stress, the overwhelming amount of information, and the understandable roller coaster of emotions were simply too much to deal with.

John Michael was laying there, conscience yet motionless, not speaking, and no one had any answers.

Over the next day or two, I found myself moving into the role of family advocate for the Nights. This was a role I had never contemplated being in, and one I clearly wish there was no need for.

Think of this: at the same time our good friends were going through pure hell and probably wanted nothing but privacy, they found themselves having to relinquish a bit of control in order to deal with the entirety and magnitude of the situation at hand. There were so many doctor meetings, nurses coming and going, tests being run, information and speculation, experts to speak with, social media posts to create in order to keep friends and family abreast of what was going on, and so much more. For me, it felt like bullets were coming from every direction, 24/7. I can't even imagine what it was like for the family!

There was nothing special about me or my abilities to serve as a family advocate. I was simply granted trust and authority by the family, and I was willing to step in and help. It was easily one of greatest honors of my life and one I will never forget.

Here's what was special and remains true to this day. I got to witness John Michael (who had just been dealt devastating news) stay calm, stay patient, and do everything he was asked to do. He continues to amaze me with his attitude, progress, and inspiration. I have no doubt he will defy all of the odds and critics! He is one special human.

Equally special has been watching Vickie go from being a mother who just had the carpet ripped out from under her family to the most supportive, positive, and awe-inspiring person I know. No parent should have to deal with what she has dealt with, yet she continues to do so in a way and manner that very few, if any, could do. The third week or so after John Michael's stroke, Vickie reached out to me to say she was ready to take things over with the Facebook messages and community updates I had been writing, and I knew she was going to be okay. At the moment, I went from being a family advocate back to just being a close family friend. It was one of the happiest days of my life!

I often times get asked what advice I have for people who find themselves serving in the role of family advocate. Below are some of my thoughts purely based on my own experiences:

- Trust is everything.
- Establish boundaries with the family.
- Know that things will be uncomfortable for you and the family.
- Know that it's stressful and there's no way to avoid it.
- Know that you will likely have to have some very tough conversations along the way.
- Know that you will have access to private information that needs to stay private.
- Know when it's time to pull away and let the family take control of things again.

Thoughts from
John Michael's Dad, Mick

I am incredibly blessed with three amazing children–Ryan, John Michael and Ben. As a father I would have never imagined, in my wildest dreams, a day like December 14, 2015.

My older son, John Michael, is as close to a hero to me as I have ever known. What started out as a regular Monday morning quickly turned into a heart racing sequence of events with John Michael (JM). It all started with a text from Vickie, my wife, advising me of texts with JM that he was not feeling right at school and how soon could I get there. When I arrived, JM was noticeably off-balance walking to my car and clearly not right so I rushed him to the closest hospital ER.

In a matter of minutes things turned south without anyone knowing what was wrong with JM other than a possible reaction to Meclizine, a drug given for the initial diagnosis of vertigo. It made him nauseous. Even after transporting him to the second hospital due to the fact that he was only the young, pediatric age of 17, and numerous tests and questions, no one knew what was wrong with our son!

Hours turned into approximately two days, although their passing felt like a month. We waited for the ultimate gut-wrenching diagnosis that was finally delivered. I vaguely recall the blur of immense sadness and the pain that was excruciating. I could hardly breathe when I heard my son had suffered a severe, debilitating brain stem stroke. Then we heard there was uncertainty if he would make it through the night and a phrase "locked-in syndrome" was mentioned.

The doctor's words echoed like it was all a horrible dream and the journey ahead would be nothing short of the longest marathon one could imagine.

I felt completely helpless and devastated with feelings of pain and agony a father would never expect to experience. John Michael was always kind, thoughtful, a true gentleman and a recently signed D1 lacrosse player on full academic/athletic scholarship to Mercer University. JM was always a picture of health in top athletic condition and what I came to compare to a Navy Seal or warrior on the lacrosse field.

John Michael's story thus far is incomprehensible. It is impossible to describe the magnitude of impact this tragedy has imparted on him and yet he continues to grind daily and clearly demonstrate how incredibly resilient, courageous, strong and patient he is. JM's story will continue to unfold under God's watch and we are simply blessed to be a part of his unimaginable journey.

To witness the love, care and strength from Vickie, Ryan, Ben, JM's friends, relatives and countless strangers has been nothing short of extraordinary. There is not a day that goes by that I do not pray and shed tears for the many blessings of being John Michael's father. I can only ask for God's hand on my son to care for him as one of his most cherished disciples.

It is, has been and will always be one of God's countless miracles to be a part of John Michael's continued recovery and amazing journey!

I will always love and be proud of him beyond words John Michael (a.k.a. My Hero)

CHAPTER 66

Tattoo

(John Michael)

In July 2019, my godparent's son, Matthew Hever, came to town to visit. Matt is a few months older but a grade above me in school. He and I have known each other since birth, but the Hevers moved out to Dallas around the time I was two. They visited us and we visited them over the years.

When he came to town in 2019, the idea of getting tattoos together came up. Those who have known me for a long period of time know I used to be completely against tattoos. Matt had recently gotten into PT school at the University of the Incarnate Word where he started in the fall. He had said I was the reason he chose that career path and he is arguably my oldest friend, so it was hard to pass up this opportunity while we were together. He wanted to get "JM24." Although incredibly honored, I wasn't about to get my own name tattooed on me! After my stroke, I determined that if I did ever get a tattoo, it would be a certain Bible verse. When I heard it, it just spoke to me, and upon hearing it, Matt decided to get that verse underneath the JM24.

The verse is 2 Timothy 4:7, and it says, "I have fought the good fight, I have finished the race, I have kept the faith."

Before you say anything, I have a couple things to say about that. I quickly realized my immaturity in choosing a verse that reads "I, I, I." It's not about *me!* It never was. I don't have to fight this battle, not on my own. That said, although the race will never truly be finished (even if I get up and walk tomorrow), it still serves as a constant reminder to trust Him and never give up. Lastly, the numbers in the Bible verse are 2, 4, and 7, so I like to think 24/7. This is a constant state of mind. It never stops and neither will I.

CHAPTER 67

God is Good

(Vickie)

I cry just about every day for that boy, and maybe some days for myself. I hate what has happened to him. It breaks my heart, but I press forward and keep looking ahead. He has come so far. The progress he has made and continues to make is amazing and has contradicted everything the doctors told me. We are not at the beginning, but we are nowhere near the end. There is that feeling of being stuck in the middle, not knowing when the end will come.

This is where my faith has really been tested, in the middle. It was easier to hope and trust in the beginning. I had no clue what lay ahead. And I know in the end my faith will be even stronger because it will have gotten us through and carried us to the other side. But in the middle, that is where I am learning to be in a place of not just enduring what I am going through but embracing God's goodness in the midst of it.

Every once in a while, I come across the bracelet I was given that says "Believe." I probably wore it for a year without taking it off, but it is white, and over time, it became dirty. So now it lives in my drawer. It still makes me pause when I see it, though. I wonder if that mother knew how important that word would become to me, how often I would look down on my wrist and be consoled by it. We have come so far since the day I was given that sweet gift, but our story is not over yet. Although I have no clue how or when this story will end, that bracelet reminds me that I am not alone. I do believe.

Acknowledgements

From Vickie:

I would like to acknowledge the many people we have met along this journey who also struggle every day to regain their lives. You have encouraged us and inspired us beyond words.

And to your parents, wives, and loved ones we now call friends, thank you for your example and your words of encouragement to us when you yourself were living your own hell. You are always in my prayers.

Kristina Daly

Jackie Faircloth

Justin Maddox

Sophie Davis

Baylor Bramble

Jake Nicolopulos

Price Woodward

Clark Jacobs

Clodagh Dunlop

To my three sisters, there are no words. I love you more than you will ever know. Thank you for always being there for me and my family.

To my friends – you know who you are. Thank you for loving me and lifting me up when I could not stand. You redefined the meaning of friendship to me.

To my church, school and city communities – the outpouring of support was and remains unlike anything I have ever seen. Thank you for blessing us with every note, meal, donation, ribbon, sticker, and T-shirt that was made or purchased.

And lastly, to Scott and Elyse Levitt, we would have never survived those first few months without you. Thank you for being our voice when we had none. You went above and beyond and I will forever be grateful.

From John Michael:

To Rivers Starke, a boy I met at Shepherd because he had, unfortunately, sustained a gunshot wound to the head. He passed away in 2017. May his memory live on through these pages.

To my friends – I can't say enough about each and every one of you. You don't know how much it means to me when I receive that random text or message of encouragement, whether it's from someone I see every day, haven't spoken to in years, or haven't even met. It means so much to me to see someone wearing the JMStrong bracelet/shirt or with the car or helmet sticker – not to mention those who have or are wearing number 24 across all sports. Special shout-out goes to my brothers Jake Moll, Jared Herron, Connor Corbett, and Rowly Evans. Love y'all.

Robert Kerr, my "stroke buddy," a gentleman who suffered a (completely different) stroke himself and is almost fully recovered. I did not know Rob before my stroke and yet to this day he writes to me every single day on my Facebook page (JohnMichaelStrong24) since he heard my story. He refers to me as his stroke buddy.

Scott and the Levitt family – for everything you did for my family early on, and for all the love and support you continue to show, including getting me videos of support from Kevin Costner, Lance Armstrong, and Chris Tomlin.

Jack Jessen – I will never be able to repay the kindness and support you and the rest of the Atlanta community have shown my family and me.

Any and all therapists who have and continue to help me in my recovery – I appreciate everything more than you know.

A special thank you goes to Shannon Vogt, Dorothee Zuleger (Doro), and Dr. Lisa Corsa. They all work tirelessly and have so much faith in me. Shannon has helped tremendously to get me off the feeding tube and speaking like I am. Doro is responsible for all the movement in my hands and arms. They both work tirelessly and have so much faith in me.

Trinity Preparatory School – for putting up with me for six-and-a-half years! I am forever grateful for everything I learned and that I was allowed to graduate on time with my peers.

Tom West and Ponte Vedra High School lacrosse - Tom, thank you for believing in me and taking me under your wing in high school along with Mark Ayad. To the boys on the team who continue to play for me even though you may not know me personally– thank you. A special thank you to the classes of 16' and 17'. Love y'all.

Angie Prosper and Jose Mojica – two of my caretakers who have been with me since I got home from Shepherd. An enormous thank you goes out to all my caretakers for everything you do.

My dad, Ryan, and Ben – you guys are the best. I love you. Better days are ahead.

Notes from
John Michael's Therapists

JM is one of those patient cases that leaves a reverberating sense of passion and empathy. It pushes you to be the best medical practitioner you can be. He makes those 9-day work-weeks' worth every second and re-establishes the purpose one feels as a physiotherapist. We are and will continue to see gains every day working as a team. Being your medical concierge and seeing you heal every day has been so rewarding. "You ARE walking!"

– Dr. Lisa Corsa

JM Night is the embodiment of strength, perseverance and positivity. The trials and tribulations he has experienced are enough to discourage anyone; however, through the time I've worked with JM, he has always had the best outlook and never has let his current situation detach him from enjoying life. Working with him has been a pleasure and a reward in itself for the lessons and perspective on life he subliminally instilled upon me. We are JM Strong.

– John Chung

JM has truly and irrevocably changed my life in a way no one else could. He has ignited a new purpose for my time on Earth by enforcing the idea that I need to make changes in the neurological community. Spending the last three years with him has truly been my privilege, and I owe him all that I have become from a neurological perspective. I dream of him walking, and it IS happening. We are #JMStrong.

– Sarah Esposito

To JM, the power you need to succeed is already within you. Every challenging situation actually brings us closer to our inevitable victory. I know nothing seems certain, and the road to recovery is a long haul, but one thing you can be certain of: you will walk again! And I will always be here as a part of the team getting you out of the wheelchair. "For I know the plans I have for you, declares the Lord, plans to prosper you and not harm you, plans to give you hope and a future." Jeremiah 29:11

– Leo Gomez

I will always appreciate my time working with JM. Although we are seen as the ones helping him, he has helped me as well. My time with him has allowed me to develop rehabilitative skills that I will use for the rest of my career in the field of physical therapy. His positive attitude, physical endurance, and sense of humor show consistently each time I work with him and push me to work just as hard. JM's ability to display all of these qualities despite the set-

backs he has faced makes working with him an absolute pleasure and something I look forward to during the year."

– Justin Espartero

From the days where he looked like Justin Bieber to the beautiful human he is today, it has been amazing watching John Michael grow and accomplish goals. JM, you're one of the most driven, committed and hardworking individuals I've ever had the chance of meeting and working with. You're an absolute ball of sunshine, even on the days you run over my ankles. Never stop fighting, nerve give up. Love you!"

– Bianca

To put into words my experience working with John Michael would be impossible. From day one when I met you, you were the epitome of hard work and dedication. From then on, you've done nothing but grind and inspire all those around you. I can't tell you how many people have come up to me to say how amazing you are or say that you make them feel more motivated than ever before. You've become an inspiration to thousands of people and I am one of them. Each day working with you is fun and exciting just because of who you are, but it is also motivating because you put in the work every single day to achieve more and give me hope that I can do the same. JM, you are resilient, infectiously loud, inspiring, driven and focused. As you know, 2 Timothy 2:4 says "I have fought the good fight, I have finished the race, I have kept the faith". While your fight is not over, your faith remains strong and that is what is so special about you. Keep fighting JM! Love you, brother.

– Matt

When people ask me how things are going at CORE, more often than not the next question out of their mouth is "How's JM doing?". You've made an impact not only on the central Florida community but on people all across the country. I cannot even imagine how frustrating and challenging it is for you to fight this battle every day. I hurt for you, and I wish it were easier. But I see your faith in God and your trust in His plans for you, and I know He is directing your path and carrying you through even the hardest of times. It's been a joy working with you over the past three+ years, and I still think it's cool that we share a connection through the Trinity family (so don't expect me to stop telling people that anytime soon). You're a pretty cool guy, John Michael. I'll always be rooting for ya.

– Katie

I still remember the day I received a call about your story and they asked if I thought CORE could help. I had never heard of locked-in syndrome before so quickly did some research about the condition. They described you as an extremely motivated and athletic young man who was currently making amazing strides at Shepherd Center. I knew right then that CORE would be the perfect place to compliment your recovery journey. You were a fighter. And you certainly haven't stopped fighting. John Michael, you're an inspiration to so many and the true meaning of perseverance. Your laugh is contagious and I sure do love giving you a hard time about the Noles. You've certainly touched my heart and I will never see the number 24 without thinking of you. If I can guarantee you anything, it's that I, nor my team, will ever give up on helping you achieve your goals. CORE will always remain #JMStrong.

– Malerie

It's hard to put into words my experiences with JM in such a short time but here is my best go.

When I was first told about JM, he was expressed as an individual who wouldn't be able to communicate. It seemed like he would be hard to work with and I was uncertain of whether or not the therapy we would do with him would have any benefit to his state of being.

When I met JM for the first time, his energy and persona reminded me of a healthy individual. Within a few hours of therapy together, it was clear that he had a strong spirit, a good heart, and a positive outlook on life. JM had created his own perspective of reality that ended with him overcoming the hand he was given. He shows his persistence on a regular basis and never backs down from cranking out one more set. This persistence has visibly paid off over the years. JM has become more vocal and directive when communicating. He has progressed with functional movement patterns such as standing on a regular basis.

Our experience together has made me grateful. Health is incredibly fragile and something to be cherished. As a twenty-year-old, it is *easy to take good health for granted. Working with JM reminds me every day that health is a blessing. Despite his condition and sudden change in life course, it was inspiring to witness his ability to progress and maintain a positive outlook. Even when we got caught running through a rainstorm, JM was able to keep his cool and find humor in the situation. I consider JM a brother and I am honored to be a part of JM's journey.*

– Michael Laing

REGENERATIVE PT AND WELLNESS:

We love working with JM! His character and the physical ability to face challenges most people will never understand in their lifetime shows a strength few others possess. But, what we love best about working with him is the amount of laughing we do during his sessions. His sense of humor, positivity, and support from his family give us confidence that he will continue to succeed in all areas of life.

We'd be willing to bet that anyone who meets JM will remember him forever; not because of his physical limitations, but because of his beautiful family, amazing ability to laugh and have fun, and know he is not actually limited at all."

We love you JM.

– Amy, Bri, and Daniel

DORO AT THE NEUROHUB:

JM has endured my stubbornness and bossiness (lift your finger, relax, again, go go go...) as well as my corny jokes for about 3.5 years now. This ability alone makes him a true hero. All jokes aside, one word comes to mind when I think of JM: grit. He has the perseverance and attitude of a pro athlete. Hours and hours of hard mental and physical work are part of his daily routine. Failure may cause a painful grimace or frown, but it's short-lived. His mind is already preparing to start over and try again.

We are all looking for that instant gratification these days. JM has been able to delay this gratification by continuously working toward a goal of regaining movement and function. He has remained constant even through times of no progress. He comes to therapy and works hard, Monday through Friday.

Though he may have learned a lot from me over the years, I have learned so much more from him, and I will forever be thankful for the impact he has had on my life. He has helped me to improve attention to detail, celebrating the minuscule changes that we can use to create function as well as to keep a high level of confidence. I admire his grit to committing to run this marathon. It has paid off. I am honored to run alongside him. The joy and laughter we experience together when he reaches a goal are priceless and so worth all the hours, months and years of hard work.

IN HOME NEURO THERAPISTS:

John Michael,

What a joy it's been for us to work with you! From favorite TV show discussions to fly on the wall awkward moments, you're always up for just rolling with things and laughing so hard your body does whatever it wants. You've been patient with our countless wheelchair adjustments until you decide, "It's fine, don't mess with it. Let's just get started!" We've had lots of laughs and interesting conversations and it's always fun to be around you. Here are a few words from our hearts to you:

From Jen: *It's truly been an honor to work with you and get to know you over the last few years. You are unbelievably strong and put your heart and soul into working towards your recovery. A mix of both grit and grace, you are an inspiration for others to work hard and keep a positive attitude, even when things are difficult. Your life is a testimony of your faith and it's inspiring to watch. I know your future is bright and I am honored to be a small part of your journey!*

From Stacey: *It has truly been an amazing journey to be a part of your recovery. Watching your strength and determination each week is so inspiring! We often work on exercises that may appear as trivial or sometimes mundane but you give it your all! Every session! (OK, sometimes 90% on Sunday after a big Saturday night). Each week we see great gains in your control of movements* *and your strength. It is apparent that your faith and dedication has brought you to this point in your recovery and will continue to carry you through this journey.*

You've inspired me to work hard, even when things are difficult.

You are unbelievably strong and capable of anything you set your mind to.

You put your heart and soul into working towards your recovery

Your life is a testimony of your faith and it's so inspiring to watch.

You're a joy to work with. You always have a positive attitude and work your hardest.

I wish more people would have the strength and passion you exemplify daily.

SPEECH THERAPIST:

JM.... where do you start.... I met JM when he was around 11 at Costco helping his dad load his car as my husband knew Mick, his dad.... Never did I think I would ever be involved in that little boy's life as I am as he is now a man.

JM.... I am so blessed that God put me in your life as your speech therapist and now over the years you are what I consider not just a patient but you are one of my dearest friends. Your bravery, your work ethic, and your FAITH in God are just a few of the things that I admire in you. I could go on! I have seen you go from day one coming home to where you are now and I could not be prouder of you. You work so hard and God is healing you and you are an inspiration to me and so many. You have never given up and neither has your family. God has big plans for you and I have seen where you started to where you are now and WOW!... you have persevered and you are where you are because of who you are and the God that you believe in. You suffered one of the worst strokes there is and you are here! You are proving doctors and scientists wrong... You were told you would never have your feeding tube removed and you did in 4-5 months. You keep proving people wrong and I know you will continue to do so. Thank you for being you JM and I admire you and your family so much. You are so amazing and I know there is more to come in your journey..... so much more!

Love,
Shannon

Stroke Resources

Supporting Organizations

- National Rehabilitation Information Center
  - ¤ 8400 Corporate Drive
  - ¤ Suite 500
  - ¤ Landover, MD 20785 United States
  - ¤ Phone: (301) 459-5900
  - ¤ Toll-free: (800) 346-2742
  - ¤ E-mail: naricinfo@heitechservices.com
  - ¤ Website: http://www.naric.com
- National Stroke Association
  - ¤ 9707 E. Easter Lane
  - ¤ Suite B
  - ¤ Centennial, CO 80112 USA
  - ¤ Phone: (303) 649-9299
  - ¤ Toll-free: (800) 787-6537

- ¤ E-mail: info@stroke.org
- ¤ Website: http://www.stroke.org
- NIH/National Institute of Neurological Disorders and Stroke
  - ¤ P.O. Box 5801
  - ¤ Bethesda, MD 20824
  - ¤ Phone: (301) 496-5751
  - ¤ Toll-free: (800) 352-9424
  - ¤ Website: http://www.ninds.nih.gov/
- United States Society for Augmentative and Alternative Communication
  - ¤ 100 E. Pennsylvania Avenue, Courtyard
  - ¤ Towson, MD 21286 USA
  - ¤ Toll-free: (877) 887-7222
  - ¤ E-mail: membership@ussaac.org / president@ ussaac.org
  - ¤ Website: http://www.ussaac.org/

Shepherd Center
shepherd.org
2020 Peachtree Rd.
Atlanta, GA 30309-1465

Shirley Ryan Ability Lab (Formerly RIC)
sralab.org
355 E. Erie St.
Chicago, IL 606011
312-238-1000

Craig Hospital
craighospital.org
34255 S. Clarkson St.
Englewood, CO 80113
303-789-8000

Follow the Miracle

If you'd like to be a part of
John Michael's recovery, please visit his
web page at www.JMstrong24.com
or follow his Facebook page:
JohnMichaelStrong24

To book a speaking engagement, email Vickie at
victorianight@jmstrong24.com.

Family

Lacrosse

Camp Ridgecrest with Connor Corbett

Julia Smith   **Signing Day with Jared Herron**

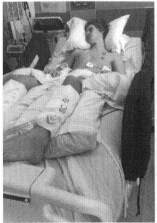

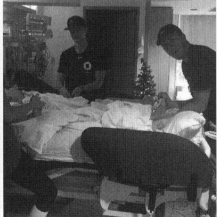

Passing time in the PICU with Adam Hale and Rowly Evans

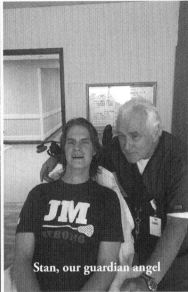

Stan, our guardian angel

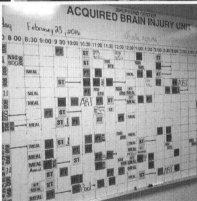

Just a few of the '24' jerseys
in the room at Shepherd Center.

Doctor and therapy team at Shepherd

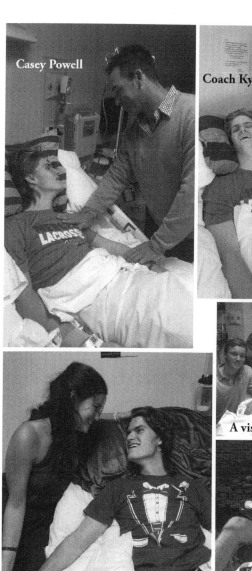

Casey Powell

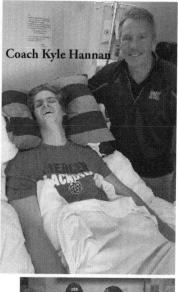

Coach Kyle Hannan

A visit from "The Boys"

Prom Night

The garden

Mercer Men's Lacrosse Team

Warrick Dunn

Kent Bazemore

Jackson Collin and
Crosby Matthews

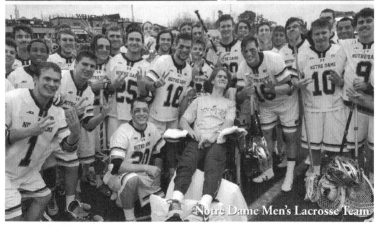

Notre Dame Men's Lacrosse Team

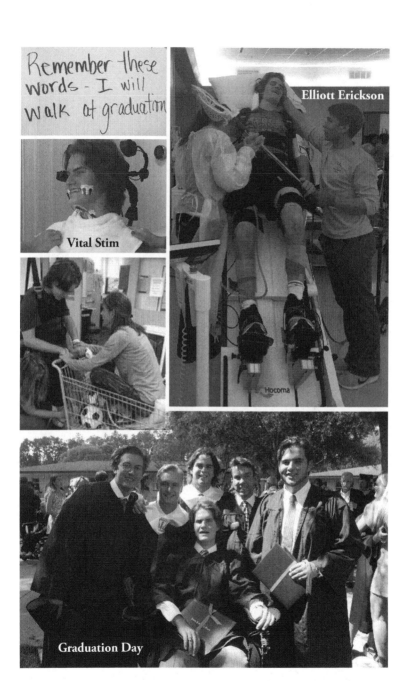

Remember these words - I will walk at graduation

Vital Stim

Elliott Erickson

Hocoma

Graduation Day

Standing tall at CORE

Mercer University

278

Rowly Evans
Jake Moll

Rachel Norsigian

Made in the USA
Columbia, SC
20 January 2020